D🐾GS
TAUGHT ME
EVERYTHING

I Know About Business

Daniel J. Geltrude

CONTENTS

ACKNOWLEDGMENTS

I never imagined writing a book like this until Apollo, my seventeen-and-a-half-year-old Jack Russell terrier, crossed the rainbow bridge. Our relationship was far deeper and more meaningful than I realized. "Man's best friend" barely scratches the surface of the profound impact dogs have on our lives. They are so much more than companions. In this book, I will explore how they can become our greatest teachers, offering wisdom and lessons even when we aren't the most attentive students.

First and foremost, I must thank my mom, Judy Geltrude. No son could ask for a more devoted cheerleader. I'm grateful that you never let any of my teachers shake your belief in me.

Thank you to everyone at Geltrude & Company, the most exceptional group of professionals I have ever known. You inspire me to continually strive for greatness.

Thank you, Jenny Smyth, for your tireless dedication and commitment every single day. You tackle a very demanding job with remarkable determination, and it is truly appreciated.

Thank you to all the clients I've had the privilege of working with over the last thirty-plus years. Your success has been my success.

Thank you, Neil Cavuto, for giving me a shot on television. You opened doors and opportunities I never imagined possible.

Thank you, Candi Cross, for your invaluable assistance with this project and for providing me with exceptional guidance.

Thank you, Dr. Louis J. Crupi and the staff at Dog, Cat & Bird Clinic of Nutley for your compassionate care of Apollo and Annie.

Thank you, Susan Barletta Boekholt of Ruff Life Golden Retrievers, for Annie, the perfect dog for me.

Finally, thank you, Maria, for standing by my side through every chapter of life and for your unwavering encouragement, particularly when the path wasn't easy. This journey would not have been possible without you. And to Michael and Frank for being a constant source of motivation and pride. May you continue to carve your own paths with boldness and adventurous spirit—thank you!

A portion of the profits from this book will go towards supporting Robert E. Williams Animal Rescue Inc. whose mission is to rescue abandoned, homeless and other adoptable dogs and cats from high-kill shelters. By choosing this book, you're not only turning its pages but also, becoming part of a story that brings hope, healing, and second chances to our loyal four-legged friends. Thank you for being a part of this important cause.

WHO IS THIS BOOK FOR?

Many business books claim they will guide you to success, but few deliver on that claim. I have found most to be uninteresting, repetitive, and hard to relate to. My intention is to offer a fresh approach with a unique perspective.

Inspired by my own dogs, I set out to blaze my own path by writing a business book that would be fun, stimulating, and about dogs. Not just because they are known as man's best friend but also, because we love our loyal companions, and they can teach us more about business than we might realize.

This book is for anyone that wants to learn about business without feeling that they are reading another "business as usual" self-help book. If dogs could talk, I believe they would share the insights outlined in the following pages. I hope you will enjoy reading this book as much as I enjoyed writing it.

THE GELTRUDE PRINCIPLES

Inspired by Phil Knight, founder of Nike, I believed it was vital to establish a set of principles that my firm would live by. Brief and to the point, they are the culmination of the lessons learned through my own experiences. They extend beyond business, providing a set of guidelines for managing life. It is my fervent hope that they will provide you with the same value they have for the Geltrude team.

GELTRUDE

GELTRUDE PRINCIPLES

1. No one wins unless we all win. We are a TEAM.

2. Nothing is random. Everything is cause and effect.

3. Always be working backwards from the outcome.

4. We have no competitors except for ourselves.

5. There are no shortcuts. Hard work is mandatory.

6. We will succeed doing things the right way.

7. We are here to serve others.

8. If you are not willing to change and evolve, leave now.

9. Do something great every day.

10. Love what you do.

Introduction

WORKING LIKE A DOG

"I've seen a look in dogs' eyes, a quickly vanishing look of amazed contempt, and I am convinced that basically dogs think humans are nuts."

—*John Steinbeck, Author*

I always wanted to start my own business as I had an entrepreneurial spirit. Having an undergrad degree in accounting provided a solid foundation for business that could be taken in any direction. Fortunately, with an accounting practice, the startup fees were low with little financial outlay. A lot of new businesses are not successful because the initial costs are great, and it is difficult to make it over the hump. Restaurants are a classic example because they are very capital-intensive with a failure rate of nearly 80% in the first five years. Although I chose accounting, I was never sure I was going to stay in the field. I figured that if I was working with clients in diverse industries, I may find a path that was a better fit and would try that direction. In the meantime, I would work like a dog to make my firm the "best in show" in the industry. Then I came across real-life partners to demonstrate the top-dog ways!

Dogs have superpowers in how they interact with humans. Their skills, services and beauty have abundantly aided our economy because of the sheer need to take care of and pamper them. Dogs are truly our partners. Often, we simply do not think of their subtle demonstrations that teach us powerful lessons for personal and professional development, and I think it's time we do.

As a view into the relationship with my first dog, we were two alpha personalities that constantly clashed for over seventeen years. Then came the day when we realized we had to let Apollo, a Jack Russell terrier, go over the rainbow bridge in the gentlest way. He was in failing health, and it was time to eliminate his pain. After we put him down, I was an emotional wreck for two weeks—something I really didn't expect. The impact of Apollo's passing was thunderous, and because I was so moved by the silence of not having him around, I started thinking about how much he taught me in our years together.

I thought this dog business in my life was done, but as the concept for this book started to brew, I also started to consider what another four-legged companion could teach me. But I wanted a different kind of dog this time. Apollo had been bred to live on a farm, hunting down rodents, herding, working—doing HIS thing. Apollo would go over to his food bowl, smash it, make a racket because it was TIME TO EAT. He wanted to take me for walks...every ten minutes.

As I stored the memories of Apollo for safe keeping, now, I needed a nurturing personality. No battles in this next phase of my life and business. Frankly, no excessive barking or non-stop feuds. Annie, the most adorable Golden Retriever on the planet, is not food-motivated—not even by treats. She is motivated by affection and an uncomplicated love language: "Good girl!" We maintain an amiable and extremely productive partnership.

In one motion, she drops to the ground and turns over for belly rubs. Annie wants a friend, a petting friend.

After all, with serial entrepreneurs, one business is never enough. While accounting is my base platform, there have been so many businesses spawned from it—each one a distinct experience. It turns out that both dogs, two drastically different breeds, could not only enrich my life but also, my businesses. And I wish the same for you and your furry partners with this guide.

—*Daniel J. Geltrude*

Chapter 1

LASSIE, MARLEY, SKIP... AND OTHER BRAND NAMES THAT STICK

"What's in a Name?"

—*William Shakespeare, Author and Playwright*

Best in Show! What to Know:

o Naming should be an intentional exercise.

o A brand name should be memorable, distinctive and easy to recall.

o A great name represents identity and values.

o Think about your service or product category and how your name may come to represent it in its entirety.

As Dale Carnegie said, "A person's name is to him or her the sweetest of any language." The sound of your name being used typically cuts through all other noise that might be going on around you. Since birth, you have been conditioned to respond to the sound of your name. Think of what an unfair advantage you will have if you're in a room and you know everyone's name. It's a strategic advantage. Names hold a great deal of power.

When we gave our Jack Russell terrier his name, we declared, "This dog is about healing." We wanted a name to reflect that noble essence. We chose "Apollo," the Greek god of healing, truth and strength and protector of the sun. The moniker was fitting! My father had died only a couple of months before we got Apollo, and my young sons were heartbroken. Our lively, muscular dog's name would resemble more than what to call him; it would be his purpose to fulfill.

A name matters. Regardless of what (or who) you are naming—whether it is your dog or a business—it should be very intentional. It has to say something. A name becomes a brand. So, what is it that you want to say to the world?

For me, because of what I do in financial services, encompassing my professional journey for many years and guarding people's financial information, the name of our firm had to sound intimate. That is why I chose my surname, Geltrude. I wanted to send the message to the world that when they are dealing with Geltrude and instill their trust in us, they are doing business with a company that represents everything I stand for: a commitment to success, service, and being the best! *Geltrude Principle #6: We will succeed doing things the right way.*

In addition, your family name is not an arbitrary brand; those before you carried it, so it is also interspersed with pride and honor. Who wants to disappoint Mom and Dad, grandparents and those preceding them, or stand for something outside the character of the lineage? With this company name, I have an everyday reminder to uphold my values like unbridled teamwork and to do something great every day.

Your brand needs to send a message to anyone who is a current client or prospect that there is goodwill in that name. That is why the name matters in my business, and that's why it matters in yours.

The name of your business becomes synonymous with its intent and meaning. Let's look at a few storied examples.

Mrs. Fields®. When you hear that name, you do not think, who is Mrs. Fields? We do not know Debbi Fields intimately, but soon after she opened her first store in 1977, the Mrs. Fields name quickly became associated with warm, freshly baked cookies right out of the oven. Such a staple in the snack food industry, characteristics that come to mind (other than "suggestive" since I could use one or two right now!), include indulgent, classic, gooey—all that makes for a delectable cookie.

Rolls-Royce. Have you ever wondered who Charles Rolls or Henry Royce were? Probably not. Two engineers, born in the 1800s, may not mean much to you. But the company and brand they created in 1906 might if you have a penchant for luxury. Rolls-Royce is a symbol of luxury—specifically, the top echelon of automobiles. Ever since their first car, the smooth, sleek six-cylinder Silver Ghost almost as sweet as Mrs. Fields cookies, hit the roadway more than a century years ago, the name has been synonymous with "inspiring greatness" and utter prestige. In other words, the best of the best. This is a name—a brand—so effective and so powerful that its moniker has universal meaning. It has become an adjective for "top of the line."

For example, imagine if you are in the business of making and selling widgets. If yours are the "Rolls-Royce" of widgets, congratulations and welcome to the Hall of Fame of business! The world knows your widgets are the crème de la crème.

So, what's in a name? First impressions, last impressions, depth and breadth of persona and personality alike, the sheer magnitude of something, someone. You could say names narrate, notify and navigate life and situations. And they should be unique to capture and maintain interest.

In creating a brand that is hard to imitate, personal branding expert Bianca Miller Cole writes in *Fast Company*, "When a company has an authentic brand, it's difficult for competitors to copy. This is because the brand has been uniquely designed to suit your core values and objectives, which a competitor will lack. Thus, they will never be able to pull your brand off in a believable manner."

You may not exactly know to what heights your business will grow or how it might evolve over time, any more than you know how your puppy will look when it is full-grown. But the name you choose for your dog or business correlates to the outcome you want to achieve. The same philosophy applies in naming your business. It is about achieving a result. With laser focus, you make the intended outcome become reality. When you name your business, that name becomes your outcome. You will it to happen. You align the universe and its energy to give you the outcome you desire.

As with the name of your dog, which you will utter thousands of times during their life, you will want people to say the name of your business over and over again so be sure it's a name that you gravitate to and resonates with others.

Whether it is your own name—the name you make for yourself in a company, or an industry, or it is the name of your business, that name should stand for something. It should represent and reflect your personal or company's brand. The intent is that you want people to associate that name with excellence, quality, and integrity. That way your name catches on and sticks in people's minds. Occasionally, over time, a name will morph into a variation of the original because it is shorter, catchier, or perhaps a change is necessary. Kentucky Fried Chicken became KFC®. Federal Express became FedEx®. Dunkin Donuts is now just Dunkin. Geltrude & Company, LLC is simply Geltrude.

In rare instances, fate plays a hand in the all-important area of what's in a name. Sometimes a person or a business will earn a label or nickname that helps secure their place in history. Think of Charlie Hustle—the nickname given to baseball great Pete Rose. It seemed to capture the essence of who he was as a player—a guy who left it all out on the field. In the chapter, "Marking Your Territory," I will give you a personal example of how an aptly dubbed nickname can reinforce a brand so perfectly, it elevates a business or person to elite status—bestowing upon them one-of-a-kind national designation.

Run With the Big Dogs! RECAP

o Your name should stand for something.

o Choose a name that resonates with your intended audience. This may require market research.

o Rebrands are tough—be sure it makes sense to the marketplace.

o Your name may become synonymous with an entire product or service category.

 Treat Time!
Pawsome Bonus Intel

Take Your Dog to Work Day is a day that encourages businesses to allow dogs in the workplace for one day each year. Pet Sitters International created the day in 1999 to celebrate dogs as companions and to promote dog adoption from local shelters, rescue groups, and humane societies. Before you dress your dog in that new bowtie for a productive day at the workplace, consider their personality. How will they respond to people and other dogs all day long?

Chapter 2

DOGS CHOOSE US

"It's tough to stay married. My wife kisses the dog on the lips, yet she won't drink from my glass."

—*Rodney Dangerfield, Comedian*

Best in Show! What to Know:

o There are signs that you've found your calling or that it's time to seek it out.

o Don't ignore constant feelings of anxiety and disenchantment—you may be in the wrong job or career path.

o Determine your mission and the universe may provide perfect alignment.

We could have the pick of the litter. There were six Jack Russell puppies to choose from and we could take home whichever one we wanted. The breeder had presented us with a wonderful opportunity. The choice would be ours, so we took time to consider our options. We looked at pictures and talked about it, comparing every puppy.

"Do you like that dog?"

"How about this one?"

We went back and forth.

The breeder was located in Massachusetts, so we really wanted to narrow it down and find the right dog before we drove from New Jersey to pick him up. I imagine our process was not much different from the way other families choose a dog. Maybe you like the color of one pup's coat, or you like the face of another. But it was after we had made our selection and driven north to pick him up that it hit me—whatever process people go through when you select a dog, there should be an energetic exchange of some kind, between you and the dog. How does the dog react to you? You see the dog and the dog starts wagging their tail. They look back at you, seemingly with approval—and then the dog comes right to you. That instant connection is significant. But ultimately, if the dog you want to select pays no attention to you, is off playing somewhere else, that connection is nonexistent. You are not likely to pick that dog.

Whatever idea you had in mind before—the one that looks like this, or the one that looks like that—once there is an energetic exchange, everything changes. Maybe you wanted the brown dog with little white patches, but the gray dog picks you through love, attention and instant attachment. So that is the dog you are going home with. With dogged determination, they select their human parent. I will discuss a different type of selection process we used for Annie later in the book.

When it comes to our career path and what we are going to do in life, we may start out with pure desire, whim or even a concrete idea of what we want to do. But ultimately, we find our true purpose in a calling. In the same way that dogs pick us, a given profession or business might be sending signals, calling us. If we engage in an activity in which hours can go by with razor-sharp focus, and experience joy in the process, you likely found your purpose or calling. The key to our happiness and success is making sure we answer the call.

Maybe since the time you were a kid, you have had a keen sense of right and wrong and you could stand up in front of the class and make a persuasive argument with outstanding communication skills. You burn up inside when something feels unjust. You sense that you could use your voice on behalf of another who doesn't have the same conditions or strength. Perhaps you are meant to be a lawyer. Follow the signs. A career in law could be picking you.

Or maybe you have always had a knack for fixing things. You were the one that could search through a bin of raw parts, cables, and repair that broken piece of furniture or electronic device that has not worked in years. Could the universe be trying to tell you that you are meant to have a life as a mechanic or mechanical engineer?

I found my calling in helping others with their finances. Clients feel the energy of my calling and they benefit from it. I know this to be true because it has resulted in continued repeat business. Remembering that first flood of serotonin while helping a small business set up their operations and finances, I realized I wanted to achieve my own financial success by helping people become financially successful. It's a win/win formula. I'm also grateful for the early signs of the calling commanding my attention so much so that I couldn't veer from the path.

Run With the Big Dogs! RECAP

- Like that initial spark between you and your dog, the right decision provides fuel to keep going.
- There are signs that summon you to your calling.
- Fulfilling your calling creates an energetic cycle of purpose and contentment.

 Treat Time!
Pawsome Bonus Intel

A dog's choice? Some dogs tend to gravitate toward one owner or person in the home more than others, according to professional dog trainer and behaviorist Sally Grottini, who has thirty years of experience working with canines. The dog is a domesticated descendant of the wolf. Wolves are complex, highly intelligent animals who are caring, playful, and above all, devoted to family. The dog was the first species to be domesticated by humans—perhaps they noticed instant family in one another.

Chapter 3

MARKING YOUR TERRITORY

"A dog marks his spot not just to claim it, but to tell a story of who he is and where he's been."

—*Cesar Millan, Dog Trainer*

Best in Show! What to Know:

o Use assertive language when describing your skill set or business and how it helps others.

o Standing out can be done in small increments.

o If you don't mark your territory, someone else will take the space.

o Intentionally evolve to stay ahead of the competition.

The next time you take your dog for a walk, pay attention. He is teaching you something. Your dog is on a mission. He walks with purpose and intent. A stroll through the neighborhood is about much more than doing "his business."

Apollo would take three steps, stop and pee. He would scamper along, take another few steps, and proudly pee again. He would then take off down the street, trying to drag me along, only to suddenly pull up, and you guessed it...pee some more. By the time we had made it down to the end of the street, a half dozen trees, bushes and other patches of turf had been marked.

Apollo owned that neighborhood and announced to the world it was his. There is something primal and instinctual about how and why a dog marks its territory. The message it sends out is, "This is not yours. This is mine! I own it." Similarly in business and in your professional life, be sure to make declarative statements. Whether you are starting a business, already running one, or climbing the company ladder, to be successful, you must mark your territory and stake claim to what is yours. It is a combination of the way you execute and the way you brand what you execute.

I was born in Nutley, New Jersey, and never left, so it made sense for my firm to be based in Nutley. My family and I knew so many people in this community. I started to inform local businesses of my service, marking my territory and using word of mouth. There were a lot of years of goodwill in this community. I did a fantastic job for local clients, and they referred me inside and outside our intimate territory from then on. Now, my geographic territory has no boundaries or limitations.

I am the founder and managing partner of Geltrude & Company, LLC, an accounting and financial advisory firm just outside of New York City. The firm is now known simply as "Geltrude." As a recognized expert in my field, I am a sought-after media business analyst, investor, professor, and author. I make frequent appearances on television and radio and am often interviewed and quoted in print. A few years ago, respected business news anchor Neil Cavuto dubbed me "America's Accountant®." I had worked hard to mark my territory—to own that space—and with that nickname, my brand was solidified.

To protect it and preserve that moniker in perpetuity, I registered the trademark, so I now literally own that title—I am America's Accountant®. And by the way, you don't have to be famous or on TV often to generate interest and be remembered for your advice or commentary.

Consider Tesla®. Tesla essentially marked its territory by its founder, Elon Musk, declaring he was going to own the EV market around the world. The branding, marketing, technological efforts aligned with making a statement of dominance. It did not matter that there were other companies manufacturing electric vehicles. Tesla was determined to control that market, both literally and in the minds of consumers. As a result of near flawless execution and laser- focused branding and messaging, the company not only owns the EV marketplace at this point, but also, the space in our heads where electric vehicles live. Tesla staked a claim in our subconscious, marking that territory.

When considering a product or service, if the first thing consumers think of is your company, or when the boss needs to promote someone and you are the first person they think of, you know you have marked your territory. You own that space. But now, you must protect it.

Whether it is geographically, or a product type, or an industry, when you make the decision to own something—and you mark it as yours—you need to protect it, fiercely. To do that, you must continue to evolve to stay ahead of your competition. Whether you own a business, or you are a part of one, an employee with dreams of doing more, this principle applies. Along your career path, for example, if you have decided to be the best at something—a specialist in a certain area—then you must mark your territory and protect it, so everybody knows, you are the best at that job or function. When you see people encroaching on what you do, make sure you observe closely, so you can outwork and outperform the people who want to replace you in your territory.

Protecting your territory sometimes means you must get tough.

I will cover this in more detail later, but my dog taught me, there is a time to bark and there is a time to bite. Apollo was a friendly Jack Russell terrier, but if he saw another dog in our neighborhood, particularly on his side of the street or close to our house, he became a pit bull. He would growl and bark, with the hair going up on his back. He became a fierce protector, as Apollo's instincts were to defend and protect what was his, no matter what.

In business, there are times when you must find your inner pit bull to protect your territory.

In a competitive marketplace, if your business or company is just starting out, you are the small dog. But to be successful, you need to be a big dog on the inside—you need to have a big dog mentality. So, when you are out there going against bigger competition, like a little dog protecting his territory, you must forget about your size, and act like it does not matter that the other dog is a bigger breed. In protecting your business or career path, you must conduct yourself and think like you are as big as the largest dog on the block. That does not mean you are cruel or act unethically. It means you fearlessly outperform or outmaneuver your competition. Every dog has its day.

Run With the Big Dogs! RECAP

- o Fearlessly outperform or outmaneuver your competition.
- o Add value to your existing product and service on a frequent basis and communicate about it constantly.
- o Protect your territory and keep a support network or client base that will aid in the security of it.

 Treat Time!
Pawsome Bonus Intel

While dogs often urinate to mark their territory, "scrape behavior," which is the backward kicking they do after the fact, is an even longer-lasting way to leave their scent behind. Think of it as your dog's way of writing "I was here" and then adding an exclamation point.

Chapter 4

ALL BARK, NO BITE?

"Dogs never bite me. Just humans."

—*Marilyn Monroe, Actress*

Best in Show! What to Know:

- Discern the right time to talk and the right time to take action.
- Use aggression sparingly; in fact, if you're doing everything else correctly, it has little use.
- Effective communication is part of emotional intelligence.
- Never forget that there is a variety of communication approaches and audiences—one size does not fit all.
- Back up your promotions and promises with execution.

Barking is a dog's communication tool. So, I guess you could say Apollo was a phenomenal communicator. We never had any trouble hearing our Jack Russell terrier, known for being more vocal compared to many other breeds. This trait can be attributed to their alert and active nature, making them more responsive to their surroundings. Compared to more laid-back breeds, Jack Russells tend to be quicker in signaling their presence or raising an alarm. And in that category of quintessential barkers, Apollo could bark with the best of them. Apollo never bit a person, but he did bite other dogs that didn't heed his warning.

Apollo protected what was his—territory, home, and family. Like so many of the things my dog did, the more I reflected on it, I realized he was teaching me something about business. It occurred to me that a dog's instinct to bark, then bite, relates to a valuable lesson in the business world: If you say something, you must be able to back it up.

Everyone knows dogs bark—it is how they talk. But let's face it, people bark too. In business, there is all kinds of barking and squawking, like bosses bellowing—do this, or do that, or else!

There is plenty of chest-pounding too, which is another usual form of barking in business. Turn on FOX Business Network or CNBC and you will hear company executives boasting of quarterly profits or trumpeting about an innovative marketing strategy. Of course, advertising is a fancy form of barking, and it can be a bona fide dog and pony show—often, a loud, flashy, and expensive way of commanding attention. It is no different than why dogs bark—it is an attempt to tell you something. But you know the old saying, "talk is cheap." The bottom line is, if you are barking, you better be willing to bite, no matter how difficult it might be to sink your teeth in.

If you are the boss and you are barking—telling an employee they need to improve performance, or face termination—that's the bite—be ready to snap. Mean what you say. If the employee fails to show improvement, you must be ready to take decisive action and terminate their employment immediately. Failing to do so could undermine your credibility with your team. It is like with a dog. Imagine he is sitting on the front porch. If a stranger approaches the house, the dog will bark and growl. It is a warning to that stranger. You better not come any closer! The dog is communicating. Now, if that person genuinely believes the dog will bite him if he walks up onto the porch, he is going to turn around and go the other way. But, if he is not convinced and decides to take a chance, what happens next will make or break that dog's reputation. If the stranger can walk right past the dog, without a problem, the dog's days of intimidating strangers—not to mention the mail carrier and other delivery workers—are over.

Because guess what? It is human nature. If you know the dog's bark is meaningless (and without bite), you will walk right past him. It is the same idea in business. Does your bark have any bite?

Your reputation and credibility depend on it. If you are going to bark, meaning you are going to declare something, you better have the bite to back it up, no matter how difficult it might be. In whatever the case, this applies. After all the barking and talking, there comes a point when the meaning of your verbiage is tested. Do your words matter? Let's say, for example, you have a refund policy that you are out there barking about, and a customer comes back and wants that refund you were out there howling about. Don't hesitate to write that check. Your reputation and ultimately, the success or failure of your business depends on it.

Biting is a dog's most extreme reaction. But there are times when it is right to bite. If someone is kicking the dog, the dog is justified to bite. The same is true in business, regardless of where you are in your career. As a professional, your word is your bond. That means, sometimes, you are justified in biting. But remember, it is a metaphor, and it is important that when you back up what you say—you bite—you act (bite) fairly and ethically.

But no matter how difficult that might be, it is necessary. People must know you mean what you say and that you are good to your word. Religiously back up your promises. Otherwise, you risk losing your credibility. You will lose your brand because your brand is your word. If you are out there, claiming to have a Rolls-Royce of a product and when the time comes to deliver, customers figure out you do not have a high-quality product—meaning you did not back up your bark with a bite—you are finished. Credibility cannot be compromised.

Run With the Big Dogs! RECAP

- Biting may be justified when it's the last resort beyond effective communication. There is a time to bark and a time to bite.
- Words matter. Actions, however, move the needle in profit and productivity.
- Back up your promotions and your promises to solidify your reputation.

🦴 Treat Time!
Pawsome Bonus Intel

Some dogs have executive presence like their owners.
Entrepreneur magazine says the best breeds to match an
entrepreneur's lifestyle, and ambitions are the pit bull,
chihuahua, pug, German Shepherd, and golden retriever.
(So glad other dogs like my dog, Annie, the latter, made it
to the list. She runs the office smoothly every day—without
biting anyone!)

Chapter 5

FUR-EVER ENERGIZED FOR TRAINING

"Properly trained, a man can be a dog's best friend

—*Corey Ford, Humorist*

Best in Show! What to Know:

o Training is a building process, and the construction is never done.

o Make training fun, not tiring.

o Professional development is growth. Don't focus on failure; focus on learning.

o Boundaries are a part of training.

o Acknowledge when the training is going well.

The Netflix hit, "Inside the Mind of a Dog," which reveals detailed emotional and scientific insights about our best friends, shows us how they can be trained to do almost anything from finding trapped people, identifying contraband, leading the blind, serving veterans with PTSD, and running for office (Mayor Max, the golden retriever, won three terms!). Okay, so what if the latter is a bit of fluff?

This book clearly serves up a generous portion of it! And isn't that the whole point? To blend savvy business flair with a touch of playfulness in the pursuit of a spirited and well-bred life?

Apollo was a well-trained dog. But he needed constant reminders—continual re-training.

Think of the training a puppy receives as basic training. Your dog will master a few tricks and will learn to obey a series of routine commands. But over the course of your dog's life, it is necessary to build on those basic skills; otherwise, they will stop learning and become complacent. People are no different.

Training is a building process. It is a learning process, and you need to treat your career the same way. Regardless of where you are in your career—in particular, if you are just starting out—you must be committed to professional development. If you are not trainable, if you are not coachable, you are going to miss opportunities and you are never going to be able to go to the next level. You also risk losing the confidence of your superiors. The employee who shows no interest in training will develop a reputation as a low performer, no initiative. Lazy as a dog.

It is important that you remain open and enthusiastic about training, along with being trained, so that you can progress in your career and progress to your outcome. Remember, your outcome is the place in life and the results that you want for yourself. I do not use the word "goal." I say "outcome" because it is about exercising your intentions and achieving a desired outcome. You control the results.

Your career is not a game of luck. It is not the lottery. You will get out of your career what you put into it. Think of training as an investment in your future. You must project a positive attitude about learning.

When you demonstrate a thirst and hunger for knowledge, you are signaling to your colleagues and your boss that you are committed to self-improvement and growth. It's awe-inspiring what that openness will draw in.

Conversely, if you are an employer, you must examine the value of training for the same reason. If I am going to put time into somebody, I must make sure they are willing to learn and go to the next level. If you are in a leadership position, it is important that you know which employees can continue to progress and be productive for the benefit of the business.

In the same way, as a business owner, or any leader, spend concerted effort on your own training. You need to learn how to manage those people. It is all about everybody being the best version of themselves. Training, at every level of an organization and at various stages along your career path, is essential. Whether that is formal training, in a classroom, or that is on-the-job training, it is critical across the board. No success happens, at any of those levels, unless you have successful training occurring as an electrifying cycle. It becomes part of the workplace culture.

A fundamental part of training is establishing boundaries. Think about your dog. You do not want your dog nipping at people or chewing the furniture, right? So, one of the first things you do when you train your dog is coach them not to bite non-threatening people and or to chew on the couch. You set boundaries. But boundaries are not always black and white. It is a bit nuanced. This is true with dogs, and it is true in business. With a dog, for example, you do not want the dog peeing in your house, so you train the dog where there are parameters. The problem is not taking a pee; the problem is where they do their business. The problem is not that the dog wants to chew; the problem is him chewing on your shoe. When you teach and set boundaries, you establish the parameters—and sometimes, subtle distinctions—within those boundaries. It is the same thing in the workplace. Take the boundaries you set for employees. Look at office communication. You want people to communicate in a psychologically safe space, but there are parameters in how people talk in the workplace. Language is a perfect example. Words matter. They can empower or discourage those around you, so choose them mindfully.

The same thing applies to the employer. To achieve the outcome that you want from your employees, you must set parameters. There are guidelines and boundaries in how you communicate with your team. As a leader, you are setting an example. The way you talk to people and the language you use sets the tone for what is acceptable. It all comes back to the importance of training. You must train your team in behavior and conduct that is suitable for a professional setting. Be the example and set standards.

In my firm, I have achieved the highest academic credentials. In addition to completing my bachelor's degree, I also have two master's degrees. I completed both advanced degrees after starting my firm. One would think that I wouldn't need them at that time, as it didn't lead to a promotion or more money. What it did do was provide me with the opportunity to learn and to set an example for my employees. This also applies to professional certifications. Yes, I am a CPA. But I also passed the Series 7 exam, have a license for life, health, disability insurance, and certification as a public-school accountant. As a leader, you cannot expect others to do the things that you are not willing to do yourself. I want my people to strive to learn more and to constantly want to make themselves better.

You never want to stifle the growth of your employees. In business, you find people who are on a different path, in terms of how they learn, and in how they apply what they learn. Everyone is on their own path and sometimes you hear people say, "stay in your lane." Is that a good thing, or a bad thing? Think of business (or the workplace specifically) like a three-lane highway. There are always people in the slow lane, there will be some people in the middle lane, and then there are those who are all the way over in the passing lane and accelerating. This can be a good thing. Different people, moving at different paces. There will also be people who move in and out of the various lanes.

Of course, there must be some guidelines. Call it the rules of the road, but you must be able to adapt and allow people to reach their full potential at the speed they are comfortable with and in the way that they think. The parameters must be flexible enough to allow people to learn and grow at their own pace.

Apollo taught me about the importance of training and continued growth. He showed me when and where boundaries were necessary. He was well-behaved but also pushed the boundaries. He was a dog, but his life helped put so many things into perspective about human behavior and the unwritten rules of business.

As you continue to grow and put value in training, regardless of where you are on your career path, if you have virtuous intent, you will be headed in the right direction.

Run With the Big Dogs! RECAP

o Training can make a rewarding culture and does not need to be boring or monotonous.

o Learning is continuous improvement.

o Focus on learning, not failing.

o Training requires boundaries because there are limitations in steps and desired outcomes.

o Results are fluid because people are unique individuals.

 **Treat Time!**
Pawsome Bonus Intel

Dogs can learn from and bond with many species and are more likely to work cooperatively with other dogs and people than other species of animals. We might compare this to cultural competence (working in multicultural teams, leading with empathy) among people.

Chapter 6

LEADER OF THE PACK

"Life is like a dogsled team. If you ain't the lead dog,
the scenery never changes."

—*Lewis Grizzard, Humorist*

Best in Show! What to Know:
- Disorder ensues when there is no leadership.
- You can empower people within your leadership style without losing your authority and influence.
- Many leadership styles can get the job done and produce amazing results—the key is consistency and longevity.

Dogs possess an instinct to lead. But there can only be one leader of the pack. Dogs understand this. In the pack, they naturally know where they fall in the pecking order. However, dogs are opportunists. If one dog does not take the lead, another will. It is the natural order of things. It is the same in business.

For any organization to be successful, someone must lead. As a business owner or a manager, if you don't take charge and lead, you will have disorder and dissention in the ranks. People in your organization are automatically going to step up or step in and exploit that vacuum in leadership. Unfortunately, not everyone who makes a move to fill the void is fit for the job or can handle the role.

Sometimes the wrong people seize power. This can be the case of "project" managers who are promoted to be "people" managers. Here, you have someone versed in overseeing processes, resource allocation, deliverables and schedules that is now managing personalities, emotions, relationships, and team cohesion. It's a mismatch. If you are short on human capital, this may be a temporary fix, but I double dog dare ya to show me how that turns out in the long term without ample training to lead people, not just be a task master on their respective projects.

People, like dogs, look for opportunities. When leaders hesitate and struggle to make decisions, or worse yet, second-guess themselves, you can bet there are others waiting in the wings ready to pounce. Some will see the leader's indecision and equate it to weakness.

Others have been leering from around the corner, eyeing for your seat to be empty regardless of how long you've kept it warm.

A strong leader will plan out a decision-making structure that designates people in the organization who are permitted to make decisions within certain parameters. Otherwise, people will make decisions by default.

The lesson here is simple: No matter what stage of your career you find yourself, leadership requires that you step up and make decisions or get the hell out of the way. Be bold and be decisive. If you can't, step aside.

Apollo always wanted to make the decisions—when he would eat, when he would sleep, when he went for a walk, or whatever the case. He thought of himself as the alpha, and so, he would have made those decisions for himself, if I had let him. But of course, he needed me to execute on the decisions!

You see, the "pack instinct" and behavior carries over to how a dog perceives their family. The family becomes the pack. The question for the dog is, who is that leader of that pack? You can see it when people walk their dogs. It is very telling. I often watch for my own entertainment and wonder, is that owner taking his dog out for a walk, or is the dog taking the owner for a walk? Who is leading whom?

Sometimes I will see a dog pulling on the leash, dragging the owner down the street. That dog is signaling to its owner, if you are not going to lead, I will! Whether the owner knows it or not, the dog is in charge. Then there are times, I see when an owner has trained their dog well—the dog will stay right next to the owner. The owner decides which way they go and when they stop at a corner. The owner decides when they start to walk again. In that case, the owner is the leader of the pack, and the dog will naturally take his cues from the leader. But if the owner does not lead, the dog will take over.

Think about what this teaches us in business. Who is leading the way? Whose vision is being followed? The direction your business or career is headed will be decided by whomever is taking charge and leading the way. Is it you?

In your career, are you going to take the lead, or are you going to allow others to decide your future? Who will decide when you are ready to take the next step? You, or will someone else decide for you? Will you step up and seize new responsibilities? Will you be proactive in pursuing greater opportunities?

If you are leading in your career, you will naturally have more responsibility delegated to you and more opportunities presented to you. Your leadership and initiative will be recognized and ultimately, rewarded. Otherwise, your fate is in someone else's hands.

Earlier, in "Marking Your Territory," I covered the importance of staking claim to what is yours (your ideas, business, career, etc.) and owning it, and then protecting it fiercely. When you permit the pack to make the decisions, you no longer own that territory. In a dog's world, that is like another dog peeing on their turf. In your world, in business, what you have created is chaos in your organization and that is no way to run an operation. Your business cannot be successful, nor, at the same time, can your employees be successful in their careers. They will not know what is expected of them. Uncertainty and ambiguity are not good for your organization.

Here is what you can take from this, and you need only to look to dogs for the lesson: if you are in a position of authority and hold managerial responsibilities, you must lead. You must communicate your vision and give your team clear direction, with specific tasks, otherwise the team will do its own thing—or nothing at all. If you are incapable or unwilling to step up and lead, then you must get out of the way.

Dogs seem to inherently understand that. Naturally, Apollo demonstrated this basic leadership instinct. He knew when it was time to step up and take charge and when it was time to get out of the way.

Leadership is hard, but you can assert soft traits if they don't cancel out your assertiveness and decisiveness. Leadership can be that perfect marriage of Apollo and Annie. No matter the combination you implement, if you do not work at it, someone will take it away from you. If you are going to lead, it is not just by words or commands. Lead through action. I will not allow anyone in my company to outwork me. No one puts in more hours than me. I do not allow an opening in my leadership. You shouldn't either. You must be prepared to do everything and anything you would ask others to do. I have set an example across the board that I am willing to do whatever it takes, at any level—the most complex responsibility, or the lowest level, like taking out the trash. It sends a clear message. I will do anything from top to bottom for my organization to be successful.

There is a secondary benefit to this kind of leadership. When an employee is called on to something as menial as taking out the garbage, they have no room to complain or question whether the boss would do what has been asked of them.

Whether you are at the top, somewhere in the middle of the pack, or starting out at the bottom of an organization, when you outwork everyone and demonstrate a willingness to do any task, others will recognize and respect your commitment. Others will follow and see you will do anything to achieve organizational success. That is leadership by example.

Run With the Big Dogs! RECAP

o Your lack of leadership will be interpreted as indecision, lack of assertiveness and ultimately, submission.

o Don't give anyone cues to take over.

o Never defer to uncertainty and ambiguity. If you need more time before the next step, say it decisively.

o Be willing to do every task your organization requires to show your commitment to lead toward success, whatever it takes.

 ### Treat Time!
Pawsome Bonus Intel

In ancient Egypt, dogs were thought to possess godlike characteristics. They were pampered by their own servants, outfitted with jeweled collars, and fed the choicest diet. Only royalty was permitted to own purebred dogs, and upon the death of a ruler his favourite dog was often interred with him to protect him from harm in the afterlife.

Chapter 7

GIVE THE DOG A BONE

"Because of the dog's joyfulness, our own is increased. It is no small gift. It is not the least reason why we should honor as well as love the dog of our own life, and the dog down the street, and all the dogs not yet born."

—*Mary Oliver, Poet*

Best in Show! What to Know:

o Desired results will lead to more results if duly rewarded. Don't think of results as a given – they must be earned.

o Rewards promote reflection and repeat behavior.

o Habits feed on positive reinforcement.

Dogs are smart. They learn that good behavior often leads to a reward. Think about it. Chances are your dog knows that when he does his business outside, you will give him a treat when he comes back inside. Apollo did. He knew all too well how to "earn" a reward. Why? Because he was conditioned. In other words, well-trained.

Of course, there are two sides to this. Apollo knew peeing outside, as opposed to inside on the floor, earned him a treat (good behavior equals a reward). But think about the reverse of that. Smart dog owners understand that a simple reward will produce good behavior—the desired behavior. When Apollo would do something particularly good, we might give him a bone to gnaw on and man, would he ever appreciate that! He would be the happiest dog ever. We had trained Apollo to do what we wanted him to do with a simple reward. We threw him a bone.

The same concept works well in business. The proverbial "bone" is not a bribe; it is an incentive that helps to motivate the employee, while producing the desired results for the business. People, like dogs, respond better to positive reinforcement. When you start yelling at someone, or start disciplining someone, they may not even be listening. You might lose them. They may shut down. All that effort you are putting in to elicit the behavior you want out of the employee, could be completely lost. But when you give someone a reward, the message is crystal clear; they received something good for their actions. People, like dogs, will think about what they did, just before you gave them that praise. They will associate their actions with the reward. Remember too, proper recognition can be construed as reward. Why be selfish with compliments?

Most large corporations have compensation models, evaluations, and success systems overseen by an experienced HR team. However, this does not excuse the person leading the organization from having their own touchpoints or times dedicated to giving a bone. Don't allow individuals to receive bonuses, promotions and annual sales trips quietly. Be sure you personally recognize their performance to solidify your appreciation of their dedication to following your vision and carrying out its tenants. Conversely, when you don't, you never know when they may still be rewarded behind the scenes and simply expect it without extra effort because the system permits rewards to fall through the cracks. Awareness allows you to think about the time to reward the people around you. In other words, when do you give them a bone? You never want to reward bad behavior or poor performance. On the other hand, a little reward for a job well-done is exactly the positive reinforcement that you want to instill in people. This is where communication is so important. I always say, when you don't communicate with your employees, they will fill in the blanks. That's exactly what you don't want.

Within an organization, think about commissions. That is the corporate equivalent to giving a dog a bone. Work hard, do well, earn more. Positive reinforcement. If you are in sales and you want your team to sell more, increase the incentives. Give your salespeople more bones, more often, or give them a bigger bone. Watch what happens. Your sales force will add a dog and pony show to their already stellar performance. Rewards can be habit-building!

I didn't need an MBA to learn this. My dog, Apollo, taught me that by giving him a bone every now and then, made him a better, more obedient pet. For example, whenever we would get ready to leave the house, Apollo would be upset—he would start barking and carrying on. We were not sure whether we would come home and find the furniture chewed on, or some other signs of his discontent.

But we found that if we offered him some kind of a reward, it changed everything. Apollo became a better pet. He began to view our leaving the house as an opportunity to cash in and instead of getting upset, he would get excited. He knew our leaving meant he would get a toy, a snack, or a bone. He knew he would be busy for a while—content— and then maybe take a nap. Not such a bad deal. By giving him that bone, Apollo was a happier, less anxious dog. The lesson learned was that a little reward resulted in a much better pet. I saw how that could relate to business. The way people respond to incentives is not much different. A little reward results in much better employees. When people make the connection between performance and reward, they are better at their job—more productive and ultimately, more successful.

This principle applies to clients as well, but with a bit of a twist. Say for example, you provide some consulting advice for a client, and it works well for them—that's giving them a bone. Importantly, you should not rely on the assumption that the client will appreciate and remember that proverbial bone (in this case, your professional guidance). You should gently hint about how your advice increased their profits. It is good practice to follow up with a client after you have done them a solid. Offering your client a little reward or going above and beyond—giving them something extra— will build rapport, trust, and reinforce a positive working relationship. When a client benefits from that kind of a tip, which they see as a reward, they are willing and happy to pay your bill! It makes sense, right? They got value from that advice.

In business, this idea of giving a dog a bone, like the many other lessons I talk about in the book, relies on one fundamental principle. The reward must have meaning. People must understand if I do this, I get that. In other words, the reward must be earned, and people have to know that there is real value in good behavior and peak performance. This concept applies to goods and services as well. You want to incentivize your customers to come back to you and get more of whatever you have provided for them. Upgrades. Reward points. You name it—these are incentives designed to reinforce a behavior that people want from you. Do this for me and I will give you that. The recipient of the reward will determine whether it is worth it.

There must be some bang to the buck; otherwise, people will see the perk is not worth the effort. Whether we are talking about an employee, a customer, or a client, people will measure the return on the investment. If the incentive is not good enough, people will not do what you want them to do.

Lastly, remember that it is important to not only know when to give someone a bone, but the type of bone you give them. It must be good enough, big enough, and tasty enough of a reward to produce the results you are seeking.

Run With the Big Dogs! RECAP

o There is real value in peak performance—always reward it.

o Rewards help form positive habits.

o Never miss an opportunity to compliment and put a personal spin on the recognition.

o Your people are always measuring return on investment (ROI) of their time and effort, even unconsciously, due to other factors in their life the ROI negatively or positively impacts.

 Treat Time!
Pawsome Bonus Intel

It's a global pet economy, and Bloomberg Intelligence puts it at half a trillion dollars by 2030, with major luxury houses including Prada, Fendi, Louis Vuitton and Miu Miu boasting designer dog lines. But let me be clear—Annie prefers me to spend her allowance on treats rather than fancy designer labels!

Chapter 8

WHEN THE TAIL WAGS THE DOG

"When the dog looks at you, the dog is not thinking what kind of a person you are. The dog is not judging you."

—*Eckhart Tolle, Author*

Best in Show! What to Know:

o When the tail wags the dog means that something is off balance and immediate attention is required.

o A healthy business indicates that ownership/management is in control.

o Poor communication and a lack of focus are top reasons for a tail wagging the dog.

o Endless distractions can rock you off balance—stay the course.

Most people think tail-wagging is an obvious body language signal. For example, if a dog's tail is wagging, the dog is happy, right? Wrong, say the experts. According to the American Kennel Club, a wagging tail does not only mean the dog is emotionally aroused. It could be excitement; it could also be frustration or worse. But when the tail wags the dog, it is a sure sign of trouble. Especially in business.

When the tail seems to be wagging the dog, the natural order of things is out of whack. Something is wrong. That peculiar part on the dog's behind should not be in charge, nor should any little or less significant piece of your business or career be in charge. When this happens, it is time to change course or take corrective action.

In business, you must learn to spot this kind of trouble. It is a dangerous time when something small or less important is controlling the business or your professional life.

When the tail wags the dog in your company or in your career, you are no longer in control and things are headed in the wrong direction. In simple terms, this is an expression that reflects an imbalance in the hierarchy of an organization or your career path. It means, the wrong person is in charge, or the wrong thing is controlling the direction your company or career is headed.

A happy, healthy dog will run around and jump for joy when they greet you. Their tails will sweep side-to-side. The tail wagging signals to the world, all is right. The more excited the dog, the faster the twitch. A guard dog on alert might rattle their tail back and forth, as if they were ringing a bell. The position of the tail relative to the ground is also a clue. When Apollo was sick or scared, his tail would point down toward the ground, or it might be tucked between his legs.

Just as a healthy dog should wag his tail, indicating the dog is in control of its body, when you are at the helm of a healthy business, you must operate the accessory parts, indicating you are in control of the organization.

There are times when the sum of the parts can become more powerful in an organization when and if leaders fail to lead. This will cause the business to drift and possibly collapse. Think of it this way. If your career or company, even your relationships, were a car, you would have to keep your hands on the wheel and your eyes on the road to keep it moving safely down the highway, in the direction you want to go. If you take your hands off the wheel and your eyes off the road, you are going to crash. The steering wheel will drift on its own, the tires will turn, and the vehicle will veer off the road—that's an example of the most powerful and important part (you, the driver) being controlled by something less powerful.

You can probably think of several ways little things could derail your career or undermine your business. Debt is one example. Missed deadlines. Bad associations. Lack of focus. Poor communication. Insubordinate employees. Dissention in a company can tear at the fabric of what you have built. Lapses in leadership will open the door for revolt. When a manager fails to manage, whether it's their staff or the other less glamorous duties and responsibilities of leading a team, the organization will suffer. When you see these things happening, you will know the tail is wagging the dog.

I am reminded of another example of how Apollo taught me to be a better business owner. When we would have a function or a party to attend, after a few hours into the event, it would hit me—oh shit, I have to get home to let the dog out! Every dog owner can probably relate to this. But putting yourself in a situation where you have to leave the wedding reception or the birthday party early (because your pet needs you) is an example of letting the tail wag the dog.

The solution to this problem was to plan better and make provisions before leaving the house. Making sure Apollo went outside for a walk and putting out extra food and water was a good idea. When we did this, we took back control. We did not allow the tail to wag the dog. Managing your business also requires thoughtful solutions.

Make provisions and plan accordingly so that your organization is strong—with supervision and structure throughout. Do not waste time or become distracted with tasks that keep you from the big picture. If you are the boss—you should not be supervising interns. Delegate that responsibility. Make decisions or put people in place to handle the things that a chief executive should not get caught up in. Create systems and structures that allow you to move onto your highest and best use.

Trusting your team is an important part of this. However, as I covered in a previous chapter, it is critical that you have prepared and trained your people properly. This is how you build and establish trust. Once you have the right people in place, given them the tools they need to succeed, and they have received the right training, you are ready to delegate tasks.

Remember, whether it is the way you lead your company or how you manage your career, the key is to be the master of your domain. Do not let the tail wag the dog. Stay on top of your responsibilities and keep focused on the things that matter. Take charge. Never let someone or something less important or less powerful control the things that are most important.

Run With the Big Dogs! RECAP

- Do not ignore the first sign of a tail wagging the dog.
- Be in control of your task or company at all times until goal completion.
- If there are multiple cases of tails wagging dogs, you're likely overwhelmed and need to make a concerted effort to delegate to the right people.

 ### Treat Time!
Pawsome Bonus Intel

Working dogs are bred to serve humans in very practical and specific ways: guarding, leading, guiding, herding, protecting, pulling, or saving lives. Working dogs range in size from medium to large, but all are robust with sturdy and muscular builds. Working dogs are characterized by strength and alertness, intelligence and loyalty.

Chapter 9

THE SMELL TEST

"If a dog will not come to you after having looked
you in the face, you should go home and examine
your conscience."

—*Woodrow Wilson, Former U.S. President*

Best in Show! What to Know:

o Let curiosity guide you.

o Look around you for inspiration and document the elements
that speak to you.

o Curiosity and instincts cojoin to make better decisions.

o Every situation or relationship can be put to the smell test.

I need to switch beloved animal types for a moment
because I believe cats have this quality locked down. To the
point that it can even kill them! Cats define much of their
life by curiosity. They fearlessly explore and get themselves
into wildly compromising situations. Sure, their instinct
is to survey their surroundings for prey and predators,
but they are also intelligent enough to collect information
for their own needs in the long term; they inquisitively
observe you, search for where to hide or hunt, and what

objects can keep them entertained. All this time exploring makes them fiercely clever and independent creatures. And maybe both cats and dogs "taught you everything you know about business."

"Most of the breakthrough discoveries and remarkable inventions throughout history, from flints for starting a fire to self-driving cars, have something in common: They are the result of curiosity. The impulse to seek new information and experiences and explore novel possibilities is a basic human attribute," writes Francesca Gino on the business case for curiosity in Harvard Business Review. "Cultivating it at all levels helps leaders and their employees adapt to uncertain market conditions and external pressures: When our curiosity is triggered, we think more deeply and rationally about decisions and come up with more-creative solutions. In addition, curiosity allows leaders to gain more respect from their followers and inspires employees to develop more-trusting and more-collaborative relationships with colleagues."

Dogs' noses are a perfect specimen for curiosity and intuition. The dog's nose print is unique, like a human's fingerprints. That nose legitimately knows, as evidenced by the millions of smells it is capable of—and miraculously, it can breathe and smell at the same time!

Even in his final days, Apollo maintained a keen sense of smell. That dog could always sniff out trouble. One whiff of another dog in his territory and Apollo was on alert. You see, for dogs, a walk through the neighborhood is more than a walk. It is a patrol. It is a reconnaissance mission. Like a good detective, they follow the scent and go where the trail of curiosity leads them. There is a lesson in there and I am sure, if Apollo could have talked, he would have told me—your nose knows. Trust your instincts.

When a dog picks up on the scent of another animal, the dog will react and respond, sometimes defensively, sometimes aggressively. Why? Because something did not pass the smell test. Something is wrong. They trust their instinct. The dog sensed danger—or something that just was not right. Dogs sense human emotions, natural disasters, health changes, pregnancy, changes in routine, approaching visitors, fear, anxiety, and more. The bond with such animals is not only gratifying in the way of companionship but immense safety.

In business, if "it" does not pass the smell test, something is wrong. The "it" could be anything—a contract, a proposed deal, or...a person.

Give your own nose, or instincts, credit. Do your employees pass the smell test? Does your supervisor pass the smell test? Do your clients pass the smell test? Meaning, are you sensing something is wrong? If you do, it might be time to cut ties or walk away from the deal. At the very least, you better look closely at who or what you are dealing with.

Dogs can teach us quite a bit about this. When a dog comes over to you, what is the first thing they do? They smell you. Why? Because all their assessments are based on what they smell—they are scanning your scent and all the other scents on your body. When we would have guests over to our home that had dogs of their own, Apollo would be all over them! He knew another dog was around—or so he figured.

His senses were telling him that another dog was in his house—he could smell him—and Apollo abhorred the scent of another dog. He would act accordingly. He might be defensive, certainly territorial.

In business, you have to be the same way. Trust your instincts. If something does not pass the smell test, put your guard up. Be suspicious. You need to be on alert and do your homework. When something does not smell right, investigate further. People can sense trouble, not just dogs. Trust what your senses are telling you. If it does not seem right, it is not right. Even if you cannot figure out why, you are best to avoid it.

For instance, if upon initially meeting a client, I get the feeling—based on their demeanor, the way they explain things, or how they present themselves—that they lack integrity or intend to cheat the government, even if they don't explicitly say so, I will walk away. I will not take on that client. It does not matter how much profit potential there may be. If my senses tell me that the person I am meeting is not interested in doing things with integrity, I'm out because I do not want to get dragged into that relationship.

In fact, personal relationships are another area where you should apply the smell test. Now ordinarily, I do not give dating advice—that's not exactly my area of expertise.

But I can tell you that it is always wise to trust your instincts. Sometimes, for example, you go out on a first date and think, well, there was nothing really wrong with them, but there was something not right (even though you couldn't quite put your finger on it). When that happens, you should really think twice about whether there should be a second date. The tangible "what if" has not occurred yet, but don't fall victim to it—we have animal instincts to help keep us safe even when emotions are hijacking these senses.

The lesson here is, never discount your instincts—especially in business—because like dogs, people can sense when something is wrong. You just have to pay attention to the signs. If we are more dog-like in our sensory assessments of other people and the places we go, we are more likely to avoid trouble and stay out of bad relationships. Put people and things to the smell test. Trust your instincts. I've never been wrong when I have trusted my instincts about something not being right for me. When I have ignored those instincts, I regretted it.

Regardless of where you are along your career path, just starting out, somewhere in the middle, or already at the top, do not be afraid to back out, back off, or walk away from a deal, a partnership, or an opportunity when something does not pass that smell test.

Have you ever wondered why a dog will walk around the backyard for fifteen minutes, sniffing dozens of spots before they choose the right spot to finally take a pee? The dog is facilitating an assessment, research. The dog is studying the ground and analyzing everything: soil samples, length of the grass. Is it wet? Dry? Has another dog been to that spot? When the dog passes on one spot and moves on to another, there is something about the former that did not pass the smell test—literally. A dog does not second-guess itself. The dog conducts its investigation and takes definitive action based on what it discovered—largely based on what it smelled. Sometimes the dog will re-mark their territory and other times, the dog will move on and never look back.

When I prepare for a meeting, I often think of something Apollo used to do every time we would let him out the side door to run around outside. He would stand at the top of the stoop, before he would go down the steps and out into the yard, and he would lift his head, tilt his nose straight in the air and just sniff for a few seconds. It was a preliminary assessment of his surroundings, of what he was about to walk into. Is there danger out here, am I smelling prey, or a predator? Apollo never walked into the unknown blindly. He did his prep work.

Thanks to Apollo, I do mine as well. Before I walk into a meeting, I have done my assessments. I will never go in blindly. You shouldn't either.

So, the next time you meet with a client, a colleague, an employee, or your boss—or before you sign the contract, do the deal, or you prepare for anything in business—think about what a dog would do.

Sniff things out and if it does not pass the smell test, don't ignore it.

Something is not right.

Run With the Big Dogs! RECAP

o You have instincts designed to keep you safe and healthy.

o Do not willingly enter any situation cold. Preparation ensures confidence.

o Don't second-guess yourself; dogs don't!

o Be aware that emotions can make the smell test inadmissible—trust your instincts, which are there for your survival.

 Treat Time!
Pawsome Bonus Intel

Dogs may not have as many taste buds as we do (they have about 1,700 on their tongues, while we humans have about 9,000), but that doesn't mean they're not discriminating eaters. They have over 200 million scent receptors in their noses (we have only 5 million) so it's important that their food smells good and tastes good.

Chapter 10

OLD DOG, NEW TRICKS

"My fashion philosophy is, if you're not covered
in dog hair, your life is empty."

—*Elayne Boosler, Comedian*

Best in Show! What to Know:

o Your brain can learn and grow as you age—a process called brain plasticity—but for it to do so, you have to train it on a regular basis.

o Successful patterns and habits do not need to be replaced but supplemented or complemented.

o The old dog commands respect; the new one commands attention. Both make the world go round.

o Resistance to change makes you less interesting and impactful.

There is a tendency to bite off more than we can chew when it comes to learning new tricks, particularly the older and more time-crunched we get. Take technology, for instance, with all the devices, platforms, phone upgrades, we are constantly being challenged. But don't ever think of yourself as an old dog that can't learn new tricks.

The brain's ability to change and adapt through learning is a fundamental characteristic, allowing us to acquire new skills and knowledge at any age.

Apollo lived to be seventeen, about two years longer than the average life span of a Jack Russell terrier. He was a smart dog and well trained. I believe he liked to learn, even in his later years; Apollo rejoiced in learning new tricks almost right to the end.

Apollo used to like to climb onto the couch, but as he got older, he struggled to jump up. He had to learn new tricks, which entailed pushing a toy or other object with his nose right in front of the couch, then hopping up or stepping up onto the toys like a ladder. From there, he gleefully leaped up onto the furniture almost with a triumphant look. My seventeen-year-old dog could still score his outcomes by learning new tricks.

When it comes to business, or in life, you cannot be afraid to learn new things. Don't ever let the dog eat your homework on this one! No matter where you are in your career, from the young intern to the senior-level executive, you must be eager and open to the idea of learning new skills. It is important to understand that learning something new has nothing to do with age. It has everything to do with attitude. Age is just a number.

The first time I was on Neil Cavuto's show, it was surreal. A guy from Nutley, New Jersey on prime-time TV doling out advice to millions of viewers! I remember sitting on set before the segment thinking, what the hell am I doing here?

Well, the producer asked me to stay on for a follow up panel discussion because I did so well in the first spot. Learning the new trick of being a commentator on business and current events helped my company substantially. I was 50 years old.

It's not always perfect. I'm human. I'm an old dog! One time on CBS, I drew a blank trying to think of the word, "blockchain." We were discussing cryptocurrency, and blockchain technology would be key to sustaining it. I went blank for about two seconds, which is a lifetime on live TV. The show must go on. Mistakes pass. Don't be resistant to change just because mistakes are inevitable. This is how we grow and improve.

When Neil Cavuto had me on his show another time and changed the originally planned topic on the fly, I happened to be reading *All Politics Is Local*, by Tip O'Neill, who wisely advised for cases like this, always have a universal quote ready to use. I recited a quote by George Washington that happened to be relevant to the topic and all was right in the world! After the segment, I told Neil that I hadn't prepared for the topic he switched to. He simply said, "In this business, Dan, you always have to be on your toes." Lesson learned! After that, I always made sure I was prepared for a change of course without notice.

Unfortunately, some experienced veterans of all different types of industry are resistant to change. There are also some young people just starting fresh out of college, armed with all the latest trends and techniques, who are reluctant to learn tried-and-true methods of doing things. I teach my students the latest methods and programs but encourage them to be open-minded and ready to learn everything, including old techniques that are new to them.

On the other hand, I am always impressed with senior-level professionals who continually adapt to emerging technologies. They understand the critical importance of staying current and evolving with the times. They have decided that there is immense value in adaptability. How about the 90-year-old who obtained her master's degree? What did she have to learn? By the way, this same woman obtained her bachelor's degree at the age of 73. How did she adapt to accommodate studying and learning at such a high level?

Dogs constantly adapt. As Apollo was losing his sight, he relied more on his hearing and his sense of smell. When he lost his hearing, he relied completely on his smell. If he hurt his leg, he didn't merely lay around. What would he do? He would start moving around, stretching on three legs! He would constantly figure out how to do things and adjusted his body. That is adaptability, which we can all learn from. Yale University considers adaptability in life and business so paramount that during the height of COVID-19, they designed courses to cultivate more of it through communication and open-mindedness.

In business, there are always obstacles to climb. Some are new and some have always been there, but at different stages in your career, they may seem harder to scale. In today's world, with technology, like AI (artificial intelligence), for example, things are literally changing day by day. To stay competitive, regardless of your age or where you are in your career, you must embrace the concept of an old dog willing to learn new tricks. You must be able to adapt if you want to be successful.

That's what I learned from watching my dog. Apollo was incredibly adaptable and inspiring. He was always figuring out how to get around things his whole life, which required learning a new trick. How to get into a room he was not supposed to be in, for example. How to get around barriers. That dog was amazing.

I can tell you, in my own career, I had to adapt and learn new tricks to stay competitive. When you think of the stereotype of an accountant—someone working with pencil and paper, scratching out figures on the old-fashioned green bar ledgers. That was how I started out. But then the accounting profession went paperless! If you survey this mammoth change from the standpoint of space and money that we saved from having no files to put in storage or in filing cabinets in our office, you see how adapting was beneficial. Without all the paper clutter, which has been replaced by a computer screen, we have much more space in the office. It also gave rise to remote work—accountants no longer need to carry around boxes of paper everywhere they go—now files are stored and sent electronically. By adapting and learning new tricks, we got better at what we do.

Meetings are another way many professionals have had to adapt. We used to meet with staff and clients face-to-face. Now, unless a meal is involved, I would much rather meet on

Zoom. It is a more efficient and effective way to do business. It is a new trick many old dogs have had to learn. There is another exception—an initial meeting with a client is often done face-to-face. That's because I want to make sure they pass the "smell test."

Remember, adaptability applies to everyone at every stage of their career. We should never stop learning and like my dog, Apollo, we must figure out new ways to achieve the outcomes we want. For new dogs who are young and hungry that come into the business world, masters of new technology and skilled in the latest and greatest methods, there is still value in old tricks because of the foundational learning behind older, proven approaches. Traditions are invaluable and preserve our foundations. When we rely only on the newest way of doing things, certain skills begin to degrade.

In some ways, technology has made us lazy. How many phone numbers do you know off the top of your head? How many people can calculate a tip in their mind? Very few. Can they do basic math? No. Why? Because everybody has a damn phone in their pocket. You punch something in, and all the answers are right there in your hand. The problem with shortcuts is that we get the answer, but we don't know how. Sometimes, doing math the long way has merit. Often, reading the actual book, not just the CliffsNotes or SparkNotes, will teach you more. There is always value in putting in the work, especially when you can see the logic and reasoning behind the answer.

For old dogs who are seasoned and smart, masters of traditional systems and strategies, there is not only tremendous value in learning new tricks—it is necessary. If someone is unwilling or unable to adapt and learn new procedures, processes, and the latest technology, they will be left behind in our fast-moving, ever-changing world. *Geltrude Principle #8: If you are not willing to change and evolve, leave now.*

To remain successful in business, you must continue to learn and grow. To win in your career, whether a rookie or a seasoned vet, at some point, you will have to be an old dog willing to learn a new trick.

Run With the Big Dogs! RECAP

o One of the best ways to better yourself is to educate yourself.

o The constant repetition of working to improve, not the quest for mastery, can have the greatest impact.

o There are different methods of learning, understanding and expressing new information: visual, auditory, read/ write, and kinesthetic or learning through physical activity.

o Adaptability is a person's ability to adjust to changes in their environment.

o Practicing adaptability may include how you are able to respond quickly to changes.

o Be responsive to new information. It may not be what you expected, so ask questions and do research to not only comprehend better but also, keep up your interest.

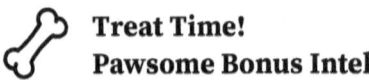

Treat Time!
Pawsome Bonus Intel

Quite the trick-prone breed, the Border Collie is often considered to be the smartest and most athletic dog. Originally from Scotland, this breed is agile, versatile and excellent for dog sports such as agility and flyball.

Chapter 11

A DOG-EAT-DOG WORLD

"Some days you're the fire hydrant, and some days you're the dog."

—*Parker Conrad, Technology Executive*

Best in Show! What to Know:

- Don't allow a negative mindset to consume you. Negativity swallows up a lot of energy.

- Peers are not your greatest competition—you are.

- If you set out to do something great every day, you can build on the satisfaction you feel with each accomplishment.

The world is a really tough place. When you take stock in how competitive the universal business landscape is and just how vast that competition is, it's very easy to get distracted by what others are doing. When your business is in distress, it's difficult to see through the forest. You're impulsive, even desperate sometimes—when you fall into the trap of conforming to this approach to handling competition.

In times like this, I remember *Geltrude Principle #4: We have no competitors except ourselves.* When you have a well-trained dog out for a walk, he does not get distracted by another person or animal. The dog is focused on himself and what they need to do to serve their owner. There is no competition. Their duties, what they must achieve, only matter in the moment. When you examine a dog that is not well-trained, they get distracted very easily. The other dog may be nipping at your heels, but you're rising and thriving. If you stop long enough to get bitten, you're in the minutia.

When you get obsessed with how your competition is trying to destroy you, you must focus on your own objectives and outcomes. Even if the competition is fierce, if you are doing exactly what you need to do (not ignoring trends, industry, environment, climate), don't give people rent-free space in your head. As much as it can be a dog-eat-dog world, you don't have to be fixed in the mindset of failure or destruction. Set your sights on your own success. You are the top dog.

Don't get me wrong; you should not ignore your competitors. In fact, you should observe them quite carefully. There is much to be learned from their success or failure. Think of it this way: your competition's failure will not automatically make you successful. Only you can make yourself successful. Whether you are a business owner or building your career, there will be a direct correlation between your commitment to an outcome and achieving that outcome.

I cannot think of an instance in my career when another's success caused me to fail, or another's failure caused me to succeed. Could there be contributing factors beyond my own efforts? Of course. But I succeed or fail on my own and would not want it any other way. I would not give anyone else that type of control over my career and neither should you.

Dog-eat-dog can be a ruthless world inside a uniform mindset that is corrosive. But dogs are not ruthless to each other; once they understand their role on the team, it's not competitive. Dogs execute tasks, not other dogs. It's really a human-eat-human world! This is conventional thinking. Negative talk is insidious, whereas if you set a high standard for yourself, think and speak toward that high standard, you can meet it and exceed it.

Robert F. Kennedy, Sr. said, "Some men see things as they are and say why. I dream things that never were and say why not." Think outside the box. Jeff Bezos created an online retail world that is Amazon based on a vision of what could be. He's one of countless innovative thinkers who have fundamentally changed multiple industries with one big idea. We may never know the full scope of obstacles that stood up externally and internally. We only see (and use) the invention.

That tough world out there? It's not half as bad as the inner world when you're not doing your best and your inner critic runs you ragged. But you don't have to feel like a toxic agent of dog-eat-dog functioning. Showing compassion is not only for others. Be compassionate with yourself and set out to be better the following day. Forget those around you, even if they are gunning for your territory!

Run With the Big Dogs! RECAP

o On the information processing highway of our minds, negative thoughts take up valuable space.

o Your greatest competition is yourself.

o If you set a high standard for yourself, you can hold yourself accountable to meet it and exceed it as a continuous cycle rather than struggling to meet or exceed others', which may never be satisfying.

 Treat Time!
Pawsome Bonus Intel

Researcher Ivan Pavlov was the first researcher to demonstrate that dogs can be conditioned to pair two completely unrelated events together in their mind, even subconsciously. By ringing a buzzer (or metronome) just before feeding the dogs every day, Pavlov "trained" the dogs to salivate at the sound of a buzzer. Even when food wasn't present!

Chapter 12

BECOME THE TOP DOG

"Success is like a dog chasing a car—if you don't know what to do with it when you catch it, the chase was pointless."

—*Michael Hyatt, Publishing Executive*

Best in Show! What to Know:

- If you think you have what it takes to be top dog (in anything), start now.
- Physical activity clears your mind for what's needed ahead, translating into better memory and focus.
- Shortcuts and "top dog" never go together.
- Know if you are more intrinsically or extrinsically motivated.

What is best? We know it's different for every person and situation, but in tennis, look no further than Serena Williams. Armed with more than natural talent and a racket, she also overcame adversity in the form of multiple injuries and Sjögren's syndrome, an incurable autoimmune disorder that can lead to fatigue and joint pain, to be a five-time Wimbledon champion and an Olympic gold medalist. She also runs multiple businesses. I don't know how much credit Serena's dogs get for her success, but her own beloved Jack Russell terrier, Jackie, famously attended her first grand slam title win at the 1999 US Open. What a fierce top dog on and off the court!

If you need inspiration from the OG of top dogs, The National Dog Show demonstrates the flair of it all where our best friends of all shapes, sizes, and breeds are rigorously judged based on their overall appearance, temperament and structure. The dogs are judged not against each other, but by how closely they adhere to the "official standard" of their breed. Any American Kennel Club-registered dog can enter to compete, and there are thousands of entrants every year. Dogs that are awarded "Best of Breed" go on to the next round and compete in a group competition in one of seven categories: Herding, Hound, Non-Sporting, Sporting, Terrier, Toy, and Working. Then, the first-place winners of these seven categories (aka, Best in Group) move onto the final round for a shot at winning the illustrious title of "Best in Show."

The dogs that win the shows were not born the best. It requires a lot of work and training to be a champion. Years of relentless pursuit. There is no substitute for hard work. *Geltrude Principle #5: There are no shortcuts; hard work is mandatory.*

Everything is cause and effect—a series of activities that lead you to an outcome. One hundred percent of the time I didn't buy a lottery ticket, I didn't win. I didn't contribute to the energy necessary for winning. The greatest athletes had a combination of skill, natural DNA, and the rest was hard work. When you start to believe in luck, it can make you lazy. Why not participate as someone who can exercise some control over an outcome? To have a formula you can execute on, gives you power and incentive to make progress—win.

While many factors can significantly influence your success, if you put in maximum effort, you've controlled the most you can in your actions, attitude, and preparation. Another rich ingredient to this formula is being aware of the place your motivation comes from. Intrinsic motivation is the drive to do something because of interest in the activity itself, while extrinsic motivation is the drive to do something for an external reward or even to avoid punishment. Regarding intrinsic motivation—drive from within, which I pride myself in having a lot of—is crucial for small business owners and entrepreneurs to learn how their own brain works.

I, for one, get excited that I have the power to link different components together to have the best outcome. Depending on the field, "best" might be relative and subject to interpretation, making it even harder to fully control, but in that quest, did you do your best? Give yourself the accolade even when the trophy went to someone else.

In my line of work, I meet with new business owners quite often. I can almost always tell the ones that are going to be successful by the end of our first meeting. Certainly, there are many factors that go into determining whether a business will be a success, but the main component is determination. They exude confidence in themselves, their skillset, and their commitment to their craft. I am proud that I have been part of the process that has taken clients from a business idea to becoming multimillionaires. At the same time, I have advised many clients not to go forward with their idea. It wasn't necessarily because they had a bad idea but because they didn't display the determination it takes for a positive outcome.

My job is to put more money in people's pockets – that could be by saving taxes, increasing profitability, investing wisely, and safeguarding assets. The most common failed business concept I encounter is with restaurants. I don't know what it is that makes people think they can be successful in the food business. Just because you like to eat doesn't mean you can run a restaurant. Unless you are a seasoned veteran in this industry, avoid it! You will thank me later.

Run With the Big Dogs! RECAP

o Have a formula you can achieve and execute on for a specific outcome.

o Know your point of motivation, which can change over time—check in with yourself so you don't get paralyzed with inaction.

o There is simply no shortcuts to becoming the top dog.

 ### Treat Time!
Pawsome Bonus Intel

The smartest dog in the world was presumably a Border Collie called Chaser. Not only did she know the name of all her 1,000 unique toys, but she also knew an exorbitant number of words and acted on them when asked. She was thought to have the cognition and development of a toddler.

Chapter 13

OFF THE LEASH

"Don't let the same dog bite you twice."

—*Chuck Berry, Rock and Roll Pioneer*

Best in Show! What to Know:

o The leash is a symbol of security and guidance.

o Fear is not based in reality.

o Innovation involves some degree of risk but never be reckless.

o Running free can open you up to new perspectives and directions.

Sometimes you have to come off the leash and run free. Give yourself permission to be a whole different animal. Innovate.

Apollo knew how to conduct himself on or off the leash, but he was happiest when exploring—sometimes it led him to trouble, but it made him happy. For me to sit back and observe him, I would immediately see how receptive he was to sniff around and use his senses.

Is it possible my business could have some diverse lines, experimentation here, there? We know how quickly things change in day-to-day life. In order to change and evolve, you have to come off the leash. Entrepreneurs who think in different ways to understand change and innovation will take risks.

I have said many times that one of the primary reasons I went into the accounting profession was to be able to explore different business opportunities. I wanted to stretch my entrepreneurial wings, so to speak. Accounting is a great foundation for everything business related. I tell young people all the time that if they are interested in a career in business, but they are not sure what their major should be, the best bet is accounting.

The stigma about accounting being boring and unfulfilling is untrue. I point to my own career as an example. There are not a lot of people I know of that have experienced so much diversity in their work journey. That is because I did not stay on the leash. I have owned and sold multiple businesses and been involved in many other ventures. I have had great financial success through my accounting firm, but even more so outside of it. But none of this would have happened if I had a narrow mindset or was afraid of taking risks (calculated risks, that is).

In the end, the diversity of my experiences made me good at what I do. In fact, I am more than good. I am *not* just an accountant, although I am known as America's Accountant®. I am someone that knows how to achieve financial success and I help my clients to do the same. But to scale my business, I spent a lot of time teaching my staff how to act similarly. In other words, they are trained so that they can come off the leash.

In the book, *Leading Innovation and Inclusion*, by Marcia-Elizabeth C. Favale, she writes: "Innovation can be a new idea, product or method that is translated into goods or services that create value or for which customers are willing to pay. However, payment is not the only metric. The essence of innovation is improvement—the ability to create something better and launch it to the world. If your creations will ultimately help others, what is there to fear on the journey? Remember that fear takes time. You are required to invest time and energy in fear in order for it to have any kind of meaning. Do you have these hours to spare or the emotional stamina to devote to fear? If you are like me, you want your hours to be spent in intentional alignment with your gifts and mission."

This statement is powerful in so many ways. Marcia describes innovation as an improvement, not only a full-scale invention in the sense of the captains of industry, which makes innovation (or going off the leash) less intimidating and approachable for all of us. She also presents a dynamic way to see fear, the big "F" word, which can legitimately stop you in your tracks from going off the leash every time. Either way, fear and courage often coexist as part of human nature. You can tame the beast of fear. You decide if your bravery will prevail.

At our home at the shore, we would set crab traps in the bay behind the house. Apollo would be off the leash, investigating and testing his surroundings. Seeing a crab for the first time, he could not help himself and had to take a closer look and apply the smell test. Of course, he needed to be bitten by the crab to experience pain off the leash. This was a huge learning experience. He knew when he had to shake off the crab, he needed to come with a plan for the next time. In other words, don't get bit twice! How will you manage such a situation?

Free thinking and experiencing failure are necessary. The more you fail in the business cycle early on, the more resilient the company will be. Just be sure not to make a fatal mistake.

One of the stereotypes of accounting firms is, you work a lot of hours, and you deal with history—report on the past. When you come off the leash and assess the historical information and knowledge about clients, now ask what else we can do to transform ourselves to help clients grow. Talk to them about trends and opportunities. Be the advisor that proactively makes them money, while saving them money on their taxes (legally). They will engage you more for the value you bring. I've been off the leash for years by being a trusted advisor to my clients in all aspects and been rewarded handsomely for it. You must recognize what the consumers of your products or services want. Clients want two basic services from my firm: to minimize taxes and maximize profitability. It shocks me how many financial professionals don't understand this.

Run With the Big Dogs! RECAP

o In your own growth, think about how you can help clients grow to create a win-win.

o Looking outside the box does not mean you can't go back to secure guardrails and procedures but allow time to explore new possibilities.

o Experimentation can refresh both your business and outlook on life.

 Treat Time!
Pawsome Bonus Intel

Dogs are often used in marketing campaigns for pet brands and other businesses. The average hourly pay for a dog model in the United States is $45.71 but can range from $10.10 to $142.55.

Chapter 14

DOGS TAKE CAT NAPS, TOO

"You cannot share your life with a dog and not know perfectly well that animals have personalities and minds and feelings."

—Jane Goodall, Conservationist

Best in Show! What to Know:

○ Productivity requires rest and restoration.

○ Sleep deprivation is not a badge of honor.

○ Our senses can get easily overwhelmed when we're not rested, especially when we have a lot of responsibilities.

○ Mindfulness and meditation encourage creativity and promote diverse thinking.

Apollo had an enormous amount of energy. Off the leash, he would run in circles, the "zoomies." His body needed to do that. He needed more exercise than merely going for a walk. Then he needed strategic rest! Our pets may fight like cats and dogs but they can teach us more about sleep in terms of honoring the hours their species requires to function properly. We humans desperately need to follow suit. National Council on Aging reports that one in three people, or 35% of American adults, do not get enough sleep, making them more susceptible to acquiring obesity, diabetes, heart disease, stroke, dementia, and cancer. In business, we also need to know sleep deprivation has a serious negative impact on cognitive abilities, including concentration, working memory, mathematical capacity, logical reasoning, perception and judgment.

In all honesty, within an hour of getting home, I'm sleeping out of exhaustion. Sometimes during the day, I've expended so much energy on a project or meeting, I'll take an hour-long nap. It's strategic. I've gone all out to be all in for a period of time. Then I inherently know to dial that back and rest in order to do what I have to do for the remainder of the day. I've set up a world for strategic naps when I need them!

Back in my youth, I was not so wise. I can remember pulling all-nighters in college for an exam. The result was by the time I took the test, I was exhausted. I'm sure that cost me a few points off my score. I tell my students now that the best thing they can do the night before an exam is to get enough sleep; of course, my instruction assumes they have studied adequately up to that point!

This sleep deprivation pattern continued early in my career while I was an auditor at Arthur Andersen. We had deadlines to meet and there simply wasn't enough time to get all the work done within standard business hours. But I'm not talking about working a reasonable amount of overtime. I am talking about not going home and working straight through the night and through the next day. This happened on several occasions, and I wasn't the only one that had to do it. There is no way you can produce a quality work product when you don't sleep for forty-eight-plus hours. This was a valuable lesson that was reinforced by observing my dog's approach to being well-rested.

Dogs are masters of how to conserve energy when they need it. Apollo was either at 100 percent or zero. When no one is home, they're sleeping. They are strategic in when my owner gets home, I must expel all my energy. You must be well-rested because when you need it, you can't think straight or be on your game without adequate rest. You must recharge your batteries. There are always outliers, sleeping too little or too much. Dogs sleep more than humans, with most adult dogs needing between eight and 13.5 hours of sleep per day; however, the benefits are the same across species: cell regeneration, immune system function, brain development, metabolism.

Besides sleep, I also sit in quiet meditation in periods of time, pulling everything back in, giving my body and mind a chance to rest. That stillness always replenishes my ability to think, concentrate, and solve problems. We absolutely need to take heed for our wellbeing to achieve productivity and longevity.

When athletes are trying to get in maximum shape, they push to the limits, and they make sure to get adequate rest in order to get the most out of their bodies. Elite athletes are encouraged to get at least nine hours of sleep nightly and to treat sleep with as much importance as athletic training and diet.

In business, a component of this rest is a break from the everyday tasks. This also provides the opportunity to learn. Are you keeping current with information that can enhance your performance in your profession? As previously stated, if we make learning fun, it's not another task to add to our exhaustion.

Run With the Big Dogs! RECAP

- o Give yourself short periods of rest, coupled with adequate amounts of sleep.
- o Just because we feel compelled to keep going to exhaustion doesn't mean we should. Think of sleep as a smart business decision when you don't think your health is on the line.
- o Energy is not endless—it must be replenished like food and water.

 Treat Time!
Pawsome Bonus Intel

Dogs only spend about 10% of their snoozing time in REM because of their irregular sleep patterns. Since they tend to doze off whenever they want, often out of boredom, they also wake up quickly and jump to alertness. As a result, dogs require more total sleep to compensate for their lost REM.

Chapter 15

CLEAN UP THE MESS (SHIT HAPPENS!)

"I've got four dogs, and I just don't do dog doo. I'm a diva when it comes to that."

—*Kobe Bryant, NBA Great*

Best in Show! What to Know:

o Messes are opportunities. It's your chance to save the day.

o Your positive attitude will contribute to the speed of the cleanup.

o Clean it up or become part of the mess.

o As a leader, you are ultimately responsible for every mess associated with your organization.

Like it or not, you're sometimes a pooper scooper. Business can be messy. There is cleanup. The intention is to do it efficiently.

If doing tax returns, preparing financial statements, and practicing accounting was easy, people would do it themselves. You need someone to assist you. You go to experts to make sure things are done properly. When someone tries to figure it out themselves, you end up with a mess. Not properly paying your taxes? Another type of mess. You must be there for your clients and clean up the mess. This is why I have a career and business. Not filing your tax returns for several years turns into a real pile of poo, with notices from the IRS, and panic that the tax man is coming to the door with handcuffs.

Our jobs do get messy. You're getting compensated to either clean up a mess or prevent one. There is no emotion in this when it comes to solving a problem (though passion is helpful!). People in sanitation are literally cleaning up our mess. What if they didn't want to? They are important functions to operate our lives. When I get up in the morning and think about potential problems, I don't dread it; I like the challenge of having to fix things and make it better. My clients and employees rely on me. Maybe you're doing a job no one else wants to do, it enhances your worth. There is no reason to have a negative outlook when things get messy. You're the answer!

If people didn't get sick or divorced, you wouldn't need doctors and lawyers. We all deal in the collective mess. Same thing with our dogs. You don't want your house or backyard full of turds, so you clean up the mess. There is a service for this, too—picking up the mess that you don't want to. Either clean it up or pay someone else to do it.

Messes are opportunities. The better you are at dealing with the mess, the more valuable you are. The reason Amazon is so successful is that people do not want to go out shopping. Now, I understand shopping is a hobby for some, but I'm willing to pay for the easy steps of browse, click, purchase, and seeing my new items on my doorstep.

From time to time, there are messes so large that we can all learn from them. I hope your mess is never a fraction of the Deepwater Horizon oil spill, recognized as the worst oil spill in U.S. history, but it's worth mentioning this disaster to see how bad it could be and learn from it.

Within days of the April 20, 2010, explosion and sinking of the Deepwater Horizon oil rig in the Gulf of Mexico (now Gulf of America), underwater cameras revealed the damaged wellhead pipe was leaking oil and gas on the ocean floor about 42 miles off the coast of Louisiana. By the time the well was capped on July 15, 2010 (87 days later), an estimated 3.19 million barrels of oil had leaked into the Gulf. Researchers are still trying to understand the spill and its impact on marine life, the Gulf Coast, and human communities.

In these circumstances, the priority is the clean-up. However, it is essential to understand what caused the mess and learn from it. Stopping a problem before it starts is the ideal scenario but that is not always possible. In assessing a mess, or some type of catastrophe, I think of my people—my staff, my clients—first. How can I clean up the mess and mitigate further damage? Part of the answer is to communicate the truth, no matter how ugly it may be, and reassure my people that I have their back. And before the mess is cleaned up; I need to be planning for the next scenario. It's quite simple—clean it up or become part of the mess!

Run With the Big Dogs! RECAP

o Messes do not go away; they only get bigger.

o A mess is an opportunity to show your qualifications and eagerness to prevent messes from happening again.

o Plan for bigger messes.

o If you've made a mistake, communicate to those who may be affected because they may be able to help alleviate the mess.

 Treat Time!
Pawsome Bonus Intel

Toy dogs were largely pampered and treasured by aristocracy around the world. Several of these breeds come from ancient lineage. The Pekingese and the Japanese Chin were owned by royalty. No one else was permitted to own one of these breeds.

Chapter 16

LISTEN TO THE HOWL WITHOUT JUDGMENT

"There ain't a man livin' who hasn't talked to his dog."

—*Hank Williams, Singer-Songwriter*

Best in Show! What to Know:

○ Words matter.

○ Discerning the message requires you to fully engage.

○ Exercise level 5 listening to show empathy and create psychological safety.

○ Allowing space for communication is caring for the person and the outcome.

Communication styles are as diverse as humans and dogs, and this includes body language when it's available for you to extract clues from. If we're truly listening, we're listening for the message, the significance in this exchange—not dialect, accent, tenor of voice—is the same as what a dog is communicating with the bark or howl.

I tell people all the time the greatest superpower you can possess is being able to read people's minds. Your dog is very limited in how they can communicate with you—tail wagging, scratching, barking. In order to know what they're saying, you must pay close attention. I found that over time, I was able to know exactly what Apollo was saying. Yes, I was able to read his mind. But how? By paying close attention and wanting to understand. While typing these words, Annie came over, put her paw on my leg, and began whining. What is she saying? She is saying, "Hey, I need some attention." Did I get it right? Well, after petting her for a moment, she walked away quite satisfied. How about that, I read her mind!

How much dog speak do you know? For example, there is always a motive for barking. It can be quite annoying, but there is a reason. There is always cause and effect in this communication exchange. *Geltrude Principle #2: Nothing is random.* Everything is cause and effect. So, listen to the howl without judgment and the answer will come to you. An employee does not have to say they're unhappy. You can tell by their work product, productivity, results, attitude, or frown. I pay close attention without judgment, I want things to move forward for their benefit, as well as for the company.

I do quite a bit of public speaking. To be most effective, it's crucial to understand your audience and interpret their reactions as you present. Sometimes this insight comes from the questions they ask, while other times you must rely on your instincts and read their body language. It's important not to let reactions unsettle you; instead, be prepared to adjust your approach to achieve your objectives. This might mean deviating from your script and speaking in a way that resonates with their interests and concerns. In essence, you must adapt your delivery—and sometimes even your message—to connect with your audience. Regardless of how valuable your content is, maintaining their attention requires presenting in the most engaging way possible.

When you have a client that is a chronic late payer, it could be their response to you not being responsive or attentive enough to their needs. You should pay close attention to how your clients treat you. Why do certain clients behave the same repeatedly? Could you step in to help them be more successful rather than seething or stewing? Behavior is not random; you should find out why they may be unhappy. Ignore your clients and they will go away.

We often hear the phrase "communicate like a boss." I prefer to listen like one. Level 5 listening, empathic listening, is intentional. When I listen in this manner, I can empathize, show that I am there, all in with their plight, and help solve a problem. My intention is to never lose a client because I didn't deliver. I want them to be happy.

You want your dog to live a long time, and you want them to be happy. This requires proper care from you. Listen to what is going on around you to have the outcome you want. This is no different when running your business or managing your career.

Run With the Big Dogs! RECAP

o Paying attention equates to problem solving.

o Throughout your life, you will likely hear many
   languages spoken and types of delivery. Become an
   expert on deciphering meaning rather than judging the
   communication style.

o If you practice level 5 listening, you are fully engaged
   and will get the most information from others.

 Treat Time!
Pawsome Bonus Intel

The Guinness World Record for the loudest bark is held
by Charlie, a Golden Retriever from Adelaide, Australia,
who registered a bark of 113.1 decibels in 2012. This was 10
decibels louder than a jackhammer and comparable to the
sound of a 1970s-era KISS concert. Charlie's bark was four
decibels louder than the previous record, set by a German
Shepherd in 2009.

Chapter 17

WE ALL NEED A THERAPIST (OR THERAPY DOG)

"When a man's best friend is his dog,
that dog has a problem."

—*Edward Abbey, Author*

Best in Show! What to Know:

o Stress can have direct health consequences because of spikes in cortisol.

o Be sure you are receiving equal doses of oxytocin, which pets can help with.

o Mental health is never to be compromised for achievement.

Inside the COVID-19 crisis, according to ASPCA, nearly 1 in 5 households acquired a cat or dog, accounting for approximately 23 million American households. The survey also revealed the vast majority of these households still have that pet in their home and that animals who were rehomed were placed with friends, family members, and neighbors more frequently than relinquished to shelters and rescues.

Given my profession and the stress that is centered on finances, let alone a pandemic and quarantine, I'm glad that pets are providing so much relief. After all, we're all well-aware of negative coping mechanisms that are out there.

During tax season, it can get stressful, so we started having service dogs come into the office each week. You could see and feel the energy shift. The documentary, "Inside the Mind of a Dog" discusses the attachment between people and dogs and how that bond can buffer a spike in cortisol, our stress hormone. The mutual interactions also release oxytocin, the happy hormone, in both species. Think about the magnitude of this for our wellbeing.

Because there was such a positive reaction to the service dog visits, I thought it be great to have a dog in the office all the time! Enter Annie, my Golden Retriever. I did my research to find the best breeder possible, someone that was responsible and could provide stellar references. I wanted to ensure that we got a dog with the best temperament for an office environment. I gave serious consideration to adopting a rescue, and I would have if I had not found a breeder that I could completely trust. What was interesting was that I did not select Annie. She was one of nine in her litter and was chosen for me based upon the evaluation of a dog behaviorist. I had never heard of such a thing, but it turned out to be an invaluable process. In other words, I relied on an expert to be the matchmaker.

When Annie first arrived at the office, she was 12 weeks old. Within seconds of sniffing out the place, Annie rolled over, waiting for her first belly rub. She immediately won the team over. Her impact has been amazing. Annie's presence is a constant comfort, and she is the first thing that many of employees look for each morning. She holds the title of "Firm Therapist," and no one does a better job!

Stress and anxiety are not the same for everyone. For example, something that makes you anxious does not make me anxious. If you have a fear of flying and you're stressed about it, in contrast, I'm relaxing and listening to music. The music is soothing. This is why dogs are awesome therapists. Annie just sits and stares at you. Your deadlines are there, your work persists, but a dog softens the time. The unknown creates stress and anxiety. Dogs put you in the now. As you're petting them—you're in that moment, and everything else disappears.

Our office does not see Annie as my dog. She's our most valuable employee because she can do something no one else can—she goes person to person and makes a difference without judgment. No human can dish out that kind of relief, and she does it without saying a word.

I now consider myself a dog person thanks to Annie. The puppy I have now has totally changed my life. She is with me all day long. If I have a difficult business transaction taking place, Annie sits under my chair completely relaxed. I look at her and it takes my blood pressure down. How can you place a value on that? You simply can't.

Initially, she was going to be our director of security, but she lost that job day one! Obviously, she needed another position to make her rightful contribution. She's a wonderful therapist, which suits her personality.

Run With the Big Dogs! RECAP

- o Take a five-minute vacation with meditation or general silence with closed eyes to block out any stimulation.
- o A dog can change your professional life through love, balance, and relaxation.
- o Stress is a part of life but never compromise your mental health.
- o Take responsibility for your mental state and seek the type of therapy you need without judgment.

 Treat Time!
Pawsome Bonus Intel

Petting a dog can benefit your physical and mental health. Studies have shown that petting a dog for 15 minutes can lower blood pressure by 10% and can help lower feelings of stress, depression, and combat loneliness. More heart? A 2019 study found dog owners are more likely to engage in heart-healthy behavior, and others have linked dog ownership with improvements in several health markers, as well as a reduced risk for cardiovascular diseases and even death.

Chapter 18

TO THE RESCUE

"I have never met a dog I couldn't help; however, I have met humans who weren't willing to change."

—*Cesar Millan, Dog Trainer*

Best in Show! What to Know:

- There is a natural high when helping others.
- Think of the service or product you provide as a rescue mission.
- There are always opportunities to be a superhero.

I have a very specific approach to business and everything else I do in life. I start at the end. What is the outcome I desire? *Geltrude Principle #3: Always be working backwards from the outcome.* Some may call it reverse engineering. Look at it this way, when you get in your car the first thing you do is type in your destination for where you would like to go. In other words, you start at the end and work backwards to where you are currently. If it's good enough for GPS, it's good enough for me! When a prospect or client calls me and starts talking about their plans, I will politely stop them and simply ask what they want the outcome to be. I want to help people and to do that most effectively, I must understand what they want. It makes all the sense in the world because it keeps you focused on the result.

Our firm is in the rescue business; we rescue people nearly every day. *Geltrude Principle #7: We are here to serve others.* At some point, we all have an opportunity to be a superhero. When that time arrives, you need to put on your cape and leap into action. All of us want to be needed, we want to come to the rescue. There is a natural high to helping others. As the saying goes, and it's quite true, it is better to give than to receive. We feel good when we can help someone. Our dogs have a natural on button for servicing humans or coming to the rescue. They find people trapped under houses and cars. Hell, they even rescue each other in movies like "101 Dalmatians" where a scrappy puppy tries to rescue his siblings after evil Cruella kidnaps them.

Shouldn't we learn from them and come to the rescue when we can? Our best friends rescue us, so we need to reciprocate. Be the hero. You don't necessarily need to adopt a dog from a shelter. There are plenty of ways to help. You can volunteer your time, donate supplies, and provide financial assistance. All of us can do our part to pay it forward. A portion of the profits from this book will be donated to assist our four-legged friends. In addition, Geltrude & Company has "adopted" the Robert E. Williams Animal Rescue to provide them with resources they need. I often say that you will never go broke being generous.

The healthcare workforce and medical scientists come to the rescue every day. They make our lives better with their treatments and therapeutic advancements. You can debate what the price should be for that assistance, but you can't deny the magnitude of the rescue. Modern medicine has been a major contributor towards the increase of lifespans as well as its quality.

If you come to the rescue for clients in your career, success abounds! There is a common thread which I see among my prosperous clients. The ones that have truly committed themselves to providing the highest quality service and products (putting their clients first) have greatly benefited. I don't mean just financially; they are also among the happiest because they are doing for others.

Finally, expressing gratitude towards clients will go a long way. After all, you can't stay in business very long, or have a job, if you don't have customers. We owe them; and the way you repay them is by going the extra mile to ensure that they have great experiences with your organization.

Run With the Big Dogs! RECAP

o Rescues have many faces: volunteering, donating, sending a care package, reaching out, speaking up, tutoring in your skill set.

o If you can't adopt an animal, consider adopting a shelter and providing needed items/donations.

o Don't take rescues to your business or life for granted. Expressing gratitude may provide a rescue in and of itself.

 Treat Time!
Pawsome Bonus Intel

A vast majority of strays that end up in shelters are pets who are lost simply because they don't have any identification. Additionally, Fourth of July is the busiest time for animal shelters as most pets get lost during that holiday due to fearing loud fireworks and running away.

Chapter 19

JOIN THE PACK: COLLABORATION VS. COMPETITION

"I'm constantly lying to my dog. He only responds to manipulation and blackmail."

—*Riley Keough, Actress*

Best in Show! What to Know:

o Collaboration and competition produce balance and growth.

o Self-awareness can dictate what you need more of.

o Avoid diversions that hinder you from competing with your best self.

o Assemble a team that promotes equal collaboration and competition.

Your ultimate competition is yourself. But outside competition can also motivate us to be the best we can be and to excel. If someone gets promoted and you don't, consider what they may have done to be successful. Use it as motivation to get the most out of yourself and be the best you can be.

On collaboration, no one can be successful completely by themselves. From birth, we need people to take care of us: parents, teachers, coaches, doctors, who all collaborate with us to make our life better. I couldn't build the company I have by myself; I need a village working together for a common outcome. *Geltrude Principle #1: No one wins unless we all win. We are a TEAM.*

Dogs are pack animals. Like humans, they are social creatures. They flourish in a structured group environment. Dogs understand hierarchy and once it is established, they play their role accordingly. Interestingly, the pack does not have to be all dogs. They will build a bond with the other pack members, follow the lead of the alpha, with the outcome being a highly functioning team.

Annie is a collaborator—she wants to be everyone's partner. Apollo, on the other hand, continually pushed me to get the most out of myself. I have spent most of my career and my life in an alpha role. So, Apollo and I battled. He often wore me down because I had too many other distractions. He had a single focus. His to-do list would be maybe three items. Mine? At least thirty! Apollo taught me that if I wanted to be successful, I had to push...all the time.

We need both collaboration and competition for growth; it's about balance. I had the experience of having two drastically different dogs. Tough love without encouragement is not the best path. Depending on who you are, you may need one over the other. This is where self-awareness is so beneficial. Do you need an Apollo or Annie? What is your role in the pack?

On her walks, Annie finds the perfect stick, fixates until I bring her back to it, and brings it back to lay at my feet, after having eyed one hundred sticks. I'll acknowledge the stick and praise her. Then this collaborative routine ends until next time.

Apollo was an alpha male Jack Russell terrier. Annie is a female golden retriever. There are two sides to a business personality. As an alpha, you must execute, be demanding, and supervise. Then there is the softer side, the gentle touch with clients and employees. These traits can co-exist quite effectively. We're all entrepreneurs; we're the pilots of our career even when working under a larger umbrella of a company. Sometimes we learn from Apollo. Sometimes we learn from Annie. The key is how to balance the two for the optimal outcome.

Run With the Big Dogs! RECAP

- Communicating a common outcome and receiving buy-in assures team cohesion.
- The more diverse your team is, the more collaborative it must be.
- Hard and soft traits should co-exist for a well-rounded exchange and positive outcome.
- Tough love without balance can lead to failure. So, add a bit of softness and flexibility.

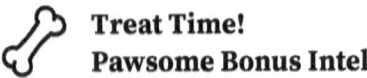

Treat Time!
Pawsome Bonus Intel

Dogs are one of the few animals who will do things for others, even if they know they won't personally benefit from it. Service dogs are trained over one or two years. Assistance Dogs International (ADI) placed 4,469 new assistance dogs worldwide in 2022.

Chapter 20

THE ZOOMIES

"You can say any foolish thing to a dog, and the dog will give you a look that says, 'Wow, you're right! I never would've thought of that.'"

—*Dave Barry, Humorist*

Best in Show! What to Know:

o The zoomies refer to frenetic random activity periods (FRAPs).

o Burning off excess energy is common in dogs. In humans, it's a little more complicated.

o Having anxious energy can lead to bad decisions that devastate your business.

o Write ideas down, then think them through, it's more productive than acting rashly.

When I need entertainment, I sit back and watch Annie emblazoned in a burst of energy, running around in circles. "The Zoomies" sounds like a movie but is a slang term for a sudden burst of hyperactivity in a dog, cat, or other animal. It's characterized by frantic, repetitive behavior, such as running in circles or spinning around. The technical term for this behavior is frenetic random activity periods (FRAPs).

In business, you may have pent up energy without a business plan, but the next thing you know, you haven't gone anywhere but in circles. Annie literally spins 100 miles an hour, chasing her tail. So, how do you channel that energy before you collapse in exhaustion and realize you haven't gone anywhere?

The reason zoomies exist for dogs is to burn off excess energy. This may mean your dog did not exercise enough. When I go home and collapse, I know I gave my all that day. Whether you're a dog or person, you should not have the zoomies at the end of the day!

Think about students who go to school and study hard, but can't figure out what to major in. It can be overwhelming. So, you spin and spin and spin trying to find the answer. You may be experiencing mental zoomies! I would suggest some physical exertion to burn off excess energy, followed by some quiet time—like meditation, and then tackling the issue. The key is to relax the mind so that you can consider all your options and the possible consequences. Remember, everything is cause and effect. For every action, there is a reaction. Overreacting or reacting too quickly leads to unnecessary errors.

What about when you are an established brand, and the zoomies strike? Coca-Cola was facing increasing competition from Pepsi and other non-cola beverages and wanted to regain market share. Blind taste tests suggested that consumers preferred the sweeter taste of Pepsi, so Coca-Cola reformulated its recipe to New Coke. It wasn't received well. Within three months, Coca Cola went back to their original formula, Classic. They were so intent on sprinting in a direction, but that direction was called one of the biggest marketing blunders of all time.

How many times can you say that you made a good decision when you were in a rush or in an emotional state, angry or anxious? I have made more than my share of mistakes. The key is determining why you made them, so they aren't repeated. I have found it is better not to react to a situation than to overreact.

Personal branding expert Bianca Miller Cole asserts in *Fast Company*, "When branding, the process should never be rushed. The duration required for branding or rebranding is often affected by various factors such as how much time your company has, the people involved, your total budget, the resources and brand assets your company will need, your company's size and future goals."

How do you harness this unbridled energy? Write ideas down. They come when serotonin is up but like in a dream state in the middle of the night, what's not captured on paper may not be remembered. Turn the human zoomies, which may legitimately come from your body's circadian rhythm, a surge in hormones, stress, or caffeine, into a productive result.

Run With the Big Dogs! RECAP

- o Business decisions should never be sprints.

- o Energy can be channeled in the right direction for productive results.

- o Writing is a very focused activity that can naturally burn excess energy. (Try writing a book!)

 Treat Time!
Pawsome Bonus Intel

In a study of 857 workers conducted by Kelton Research for Banfield Pet Hospital, an astounding 93% of the C-suite executives surveyed grew up with a pet, and 78% partially attribute their career success in part to owning a pet as a child. Nearly a quarter (24%) say that their childhood pet taught them more valuable lessons than their first internship. A whopping 77% of C-suite executives said they came up with a business idea while walking a pet.

DOUBLE DOG DARE— COMEBACKS

"A puppy plays with every pup he meets,
but an old dog has few associates."

—Josh Billings, Humorist

Best in Show! What to Know:

- Detours from your dream do not have to be a death sentence.
- Look to examples of comebacks for inspiration.
- Resilience is the greatest trait that comebacks can spring from.
- Something that feels unexpected or miserable can be a blessing in disguise.
- As the occasion arises, take the rare opportunity to reinvent yourself and come out as a better version.

We prepared ourselves several times to lose our beloved dog. Apollo had lost his hearing, and his eyesight deteriorated. He had experienced significant issues with his back with all that extreme jumping and physical activity.

As his energy wavered and his face grew listless, suddenly he would spring into youthfulness again, like doggy time travel. Instead of "Back to the Future," it was back to health! Repeatedly. Apollo mastered that art of the comeback.

Not long after I started my firm, my largest client, Chart House Restaurant in Weehawken, New Jersey experienced a fire, and the establishment completely burned to the ground. Nothing was left but smoke and ashes. The business was completely wiped out, but they licked their wounds, rebuilt, and made their business better than ever. It was a terrible situation for many reasons, but in their reconstruction, they rehired many of their employees, who came back energized. Their energy helped the business thrive. Anytime a business experiences a fire, even if it does not destroy the building, the smoke damage alone can cause the need to knock it all down. It takes a lot of fortitude to come back from that. When you see your hopes and dreams go up and smoke, you must be able to see the silver lining to see what could be beyond the disaster. *Geltrude Principle #8: If you are not willing to change and evolve, leave now.*

When Chart House burned down, I had serious questions about whether my business would survive. I had only been in business for about two years at the time. I had also just purchased a new home that was going to require significant renovations. After realizing the vision of owning my own business, I was thinking that it might not be meant to be and that I would have to go out and get a job. But I didn't give up on my dreams and became even more determined to succeed.

I've been in situations multiple times where we lost a large client due to circumstances beyond our control. Therefore, I needed to build my company so we didn't depend on any one client for a significant share of the revenue. Part of the comeback is continuing to shape and reshape. This is professional maturity.

Samsung's Galaxy Note 7, while popular when released in 2016, soon faced serious public relations challenges. The issue wasn't due to a short battery life. The batteries exploded in some cases or set themselves ablaze in others. The cause of what CNet referred to as "one of history's worst tech product recalls," was eventually revealed by the manufacturer a year after the initial nightmare—yes, the batteries were to blame. The recall replacement batteries, from a third-party manufacturer, could catch fire in your front pocket too!

The widespread issue not only led to a global recall; it also caused consumer safety concerns and financial losses. The original battery had a design flaw, and the replacements suffered from a rushed lack of safety measures while trying to meet demand.

Multi-tiered global recall (implementing a PR strategy that made improvements and accountability front and center) enhanced safety testing and changes to third-party suppliers. By addressing the problem head-on with new and improved safety protocols, Samsung underscored its commitment to consumer welfare and was able to move past the issues (and resulting jokes), albeit with substantial financial setbacks.

Run With the Big Dogs! RECAP

- ○ It's not over until it's truly over. Ask yourself what action you can take to change course?

- ○ When planning a comeback, focus on changing and evolving rather than returning to the original version.

- ○ All is never truly lost; the new space you find may be the gain you need.

 Treat Time!
Pawsome Bonus Intel

Like humans, dogs that are bold, sociable, and exhibit emotional and inhibitory control are more likely to be resilient. They should also be able to adapt to change and be flexible. Bobi, "oldest dog ever," according to Guinness World Records, had lived a record-breaking 31 years and 165 days old when he died in October 2023.

Chapter 22

DELEGATE TO THE DOG WHISPERERS

"I've been on so many blind dates, I should get a free dog."

—*Wendy Liebman, Comedian*

Best in Show! What to Know:

- People possess a variety of skills and talents that you don't.

- Understand what others around you are good at and how they can help you.

- Sight is usually the first sense we use to make spur-of-the-moment decisions whether we have aptitude to make the decision or not. Pause!

- Delegation frees you up to serve in your highest and best use.

The Peter Principle is a concept in management developed by Laurence J. Peter, which observes that people in a hierarchy tend to rise to "a level of respective incompetence": employees are promoted based on their success in previous jobs until they reach a level at which they are no longer competent, as skills in one job do not necessarily translate to another. When you think about it, people should be in the position which best suits their skillset.

Say you are an airline mechanic, so you fix engines on airplanes, and you are the best at what you do. Because you perform so well in your position, you get promoted to be a supervisor and no longer work directly on engines. Instead, you are responsible for overseeing others, but you are not a people person. Your promotion has put you in a position that has a high likelihood of failure. It doesn't make sense, but it happens all the time.

Much of the success I have had in my career is based upon who I have surrounded myself with inside and outside of my company. I have never felt threatened by having intelligent and talented people working for me. I don't want to be the smartest person at Geltrude & Company. I want to lead the best and the brightest. In addition, I have always hired the best possible consultants, attorneys, and advisers to guide me. I trust them to do what they do, so I can do what I do.

In delegation, we need to understand what others are better at. For me to be able to spend my time doing what I do best, I must hire others with complementary skillsets. To succeed, you must recognize when this principle applies.

I spent over seventeen years with Apollo and did plenty of research and reading about dogs during that time. However, I understood that there were experts that could recommend the dog that would be the perfect complement to my life. So that is what I was searching for before I found

Annie. It is important to be surrounded by people, and pets, who complement our lives perfectly.

When I traveled to see a new litter of Golden Retrievers, our dog whisperer, Susan Barletta Boekholt, recognized me from TV, which helped build an immediate rapport. All the pups looked the same: adorable! But I decided to get my dog from her because I loved her approach to finding homes for her pups. She analyzes the personality of each puppy and matches them with your wish list: no yapping, abundance of friendliness and contentment, etc. She FaceTimed me after the behavior evaluation, and beamed, "We found your dog!" holding up a ball of fur to the camera.

Why should I have picked the dog when I could lean on someone who is an expert? It could have been an instant mismatch, and the chances of unhappiness, imbalance in the household (and workplace, in my case) was an unnecessary risk in these circumstances. I say it is better to delegate to an expert that you trust than to be carried away by the force of love at first sight, which can be overwhelming.

The shiny object always beckons but pause for the cause—and think about the outcome you desire.

Run With the Big Dogs! RECAP

o Spontaneous decisions can cause long-term consequences.

o Delegate to others to spread the responsibilities where best matched.

o Hiring people with diverse skillsets fosters positive exchanges that show the strength and wisdom of your choices.

 Treat Time!
Pawsome Bonus Intel

Are dogs more discerning than businesspeople? Neuroscience is delving deeply into the incredible number of signals we humans send to one another through our energy, our intentions and our body language and tone. So much of what we convey comes not from the specific words, but the context. Dog Whisperer Cesar Milan said that dogs would refuse to follow dogs with negative or unbalanced energy, whereas humans will to their detriment.

Chapter 23

DON'T JUDGE A DOG BY ITS COAT

"But was there ever a dog that praised his fleas?"

—William Butler Yeats, Poet

Best in Show! What to Know:

o Mindset is a game changer, especially when starting out, as you will be judged for inexperience.

o Small size, big fight can make you a top dog...eventually.

o Founders started somewhere; many in messy garages or bedrooms.

o Most actions and reactions can be divided into the pain or pleasure category.

What a cute, adorable puppy! We had two sons at the time that were quite active, so we thought they would wear Apollo out. The opposite occurred. Apollo turned out to be a ball of muscle with incredible stamina.

I viewed Apollo as strong and confident. I believe he saw himself as much larger than he was. He only weighed thirty pounds, but he wouldn't take shit from any dog, no matter if it was a Rottweiler or German Sheppard. He viewed himself as a big dog with a big dog attitude, and other dogs sensed that about him. So much so that larger dogs shied away from him.

In starting my accounting and financial services firm as this small entity to be where we are now—a mid-sized firm driving toward becoming a large firm—our mindset of who we are never wavers. We have the discipline to become a large firm. If your view is small, you will remain small. Mentality is always a game changer. Numerous giant companies have started out of garages. If they didn't have the fight inside them to believe in what they could be, and conduct themselves in that manner, they would be small, period. Our clients who became successful business owners all have the same story—small size, big fight.

Jack Russell terriers are known for being big dogs trapped inside small bodies. They carry themselves in a specific way. Apollo was off the leash inside our property. He knew how far he could go. As he exerted himself and the size of his fight, other dogs would lead their owners away! The competition will back off when you showcase that type of fight.

When people hear that I'm an accountant, immediately they go to stereotypes. But that is NOT me. Accountants take history and put the data in the right columns. It's a necessary evil to prepare a financial statement or tax return. My approach is to tell you what those numbers mean and what you should do next to have more money in your pocket. I look at real estate, the stock market, everything going on around the world so I can take my client's situation and provide the greatest path to success. Yes, I'll say it—I predict the future!

There are two things people want; everything we do as humans arises out of avoiding pain and/or seeking pleasure. Now how do I translate that feeling into my business? I can't make it complicated. Long, flowery mission statements do not signify action. I use four words to translate that into my business: "Minimizing Taxes, Maximizing Profitability." If you have a business, this means I will help you reduce your taxes and adopt a business model that makes you more successful. *Geltrude Principle #10: Love what you do.* When you like what you do, you can become good at it. When you love what you do, you can become the best. I truly believe that my firm is the best at what we do.

What do clients want to move away from? What will make them happy? I'm utilizing level 5 listening and then responding accordingly. When I deliver on this, they're a client for life. This principle is not limited to companies. You want to be around people (and dogs) who make you happy (or teach you about business)!

Run With the Big Dogs! RECAP

o Feelings play a huge role in business, even repressed ones.

o Beauty fades, but a strong attitude can take you quite far.

o Make sure that beautiful coat is backed up by the right bark and bite.

 Treat Time!
Pawsome Bonus Intel

There are alleged personality differences between individuals who self-identify as "dog people" and "cat people." Yet studies offer a rather conflicting picture of what personality differences, if any, exist between the two types. Using a publicly accessible website, 4,565 participants completed the Big Five Inventory and self-identified as a dog person, cat person, both, or neither. Results suggest that dog people are higher on extraversion, agreeableness, and conscientiousness, but lower on neuroticism and openness than are cat people.

ABOUT THE AUTHOR

Daniel J. Geltrude, CPA is the founder and managing member of Geltrude & Company, LLC, an innovative accounting and financial services firm. Although Dan is known as "America's Accountant®" he is far more than just an accountant. He is an equity investor, real estate expert, college professor, bank founder, bestselling author, profitability consultant and much more. It has been said that he is a renaissance man when it comes to financial knowledge, creative thinking, and communication. Dan can be seen on national cable networks providing insight on financial, tax, economic, market and political matters. A clear and concise speaker, audiences especially love his interpretation of how political policies and events impact their wallets.

Dan is the author of *Dogs Taught Me Everything I Know About Business* and *Positive Financial Karma*.

REFERENCES

ASPCA Pro. "New ASPCA Survey: Vast Majority of Dogs and Cats Acquired During Pandemic Still in Their Homes." ASPCA Pro. https://www.aspcapro.org/resource/new-aspca-survey-vast-majority-dogs-and-cats-acquired-during-pandemic-still-their-homes.

Assistance Dogs International. "2022 Fact Sheet." Assistance Dogs International. https://assistancedogsinternational.org/clientuploads/ADI%20 Business/2022_ADI_Fact_Sheet.pdf.

Bahl, Sugandh. "Entrepreneurs Talk About How Their Pets Make Their Lives Better." *Entrepreneur.* December 3, 2017. https://www.entrepreneur.com/en-in/lifestyle/entrepreneurs-talk- about-how-their-pets-make-their-lives/305562.

Bileta, Vedra. "Dogs in Ancient Egypt: The Early Origins of Man's Best Friend." *The Collector.* January 1, 2023. https://www.thecollector.com/dogs-in-ancient-egypt/.

Bloom, Mary. "What's the Difference Between the Pekingese and the Japanese Chin?" *Modern Dog.* December 21, 2023. https://moderndogmagazine.com/articles/whats-the-difference-between-the-pekingese-and-the-japanese-chin/.

Bloomberg. "Global Pet Industry To Grow To $500 Billion By 2030, Bloomberg Intelligence Report Finds." *Bloomberg.* March 24, 2023.

https://www.bloomberg.com/company/press/global-pet-industry-to-grow-to-500-billion-by-2030-bloomberg-intelligence-finds/.

Chao, Ray. "Working Dog Spotlight: Dog Actors." *Pets Best.* October 14, 2020. https://www.petsbest.com/blog/working-as-dog-actors#:~:text=How%20much%20do%20dog%20actors,for%20a%20non%2Dunion%20commercial.

Cole, Bianca Miller. "How Do Branding Processes Work And How Long Do They Take?" *Forbes.* December 10, 2018. https://www.forbes.com/sites/biancamillercole/2018/12/10/how-do-branding-processes-work-and-how-long-do-they-take/.

Cooper, Anderson. "The Smartest Dog in the World." *CBS News.* August 16, 2018. https://www.cbsnews.com/news/smart-dog-anderson-cooper-60- minutes-chaser-8-16-18/.

Cornell Richard P. Riney Canine Health Center. "What are zoomies?" Cornell Richard P. Riney Canine Health Center. https://www.vet.cornell.edu/departments-centers-and-institutes/riney-canine-health-center/canine-health-information/what-are-zoomies.

Dogtime Staff. "Retriever earns world record for his bark." *Dogtime.* March 15, 2013. https://dogtime.com/dog-blog/trending/17455-retriever-earns-world-record-for-his-bark.

DuVernet, Dia. "When your dog takes a snooze, they may be dreaming about you." Pasadena Humane. July 31, 2024.

Favale, Marcia-Elizabeth C. *Leading Innovation and Inclusion.* New York, New York: M. Favale-Tarter LLC. July 2024.

Finlay, Katie. "Can Dogs Taste?" American Kennel Club. March 19, 2018.
https://www.akc.org/expert-advice/lifestyle/can-dogs-taste/#:~:text=A%20dog's%20sense%20of%20taste%20is%20much%20less%20discriminating%20than,sixth%20as%20powerful%20as%20ours.

From Way Downtown. "Michael Jordan: The Real No. 1 Draft Choice, 1984." *Pro Basketball History Blog.*
https://from-way-downtown.com/2023/01/09/michael-jordan-the-real-no-1-draft-choice-1984/.

Gaba, Ripunjay. "All About Serena Williams' Dogs." *Essentially Sports.* March 17, 2023.
https://www.essentiallysports.com/wta-tennis-news-stable-all-about-serena-williams-dogs/.

Gino, Francesco. "The Business Case for Curiosity." *Harvard Business Review.* September-October 2018.
https://hbr.org/2018/09/the-business-case-for-curiosity.

Gosling, S. D., Sandy, C. J., & Potter, J. (2010). "Personalities of self-identified 'dog people' and 'cat people'." *Anthrozoös,* 23(3), 213-222.

iNaturalist. "Dog." *iNaturalist Guide.*
https://www.inaturalist.org/guide_taxa/223550.

Jowaheer, Roshina. "How petting a dog can lower your blood pressure by 10%." *Country Living*. September 28, 2018. https://www.countryliving.com/uk/wellbeing/a23503266/petting-dog-lowers-blood-pressure/.

Kleenex.
https://www.kleenex.com/en-us/.

Klein, Christopher. "Why Coca-Cola's 'New Coke' Flopped." *History.com*. September 14, 2023. https://www.history.com/news/why-coca-cola-new-coke-flopped.

Leader Who Leads. "Levels of Listening." *LeaderWhoLeads. com*.https://www.leaderwholeads.com/levels-of-listening.html#:~:text=Level%205%3A%20Empathic%20Listening,truly%20 hear%20the%20other%20person.

Leib, Mason. "90-year-old woman becomes oldest person to complete master's degree at Texas university." *GMA/ABC News*. December 19, 2023. https://abcnews.go.com/GMA/Living/90-year-woman-oldest-person- complete-masters-degree/story?id=105774145.

Locker, Melissa. "Want to be a Successful CEO? Get a Dog." *Fast Company*. November 15, 2018. https://www.fastcompany.com/90268052/new-survey-links-pet- ownership-to-professional-success.

Lopez, Maribel. "Samsung Explains Note 7 Battery Explosions and Turns Crisis Into Opportunity." *Forbes*. January 22, 2017.

https://www.forbes.com/sites/maribellopez/2017/01/22/ samsung- reveals-cause-of-note-7-issue-turns-crisis-into- opportunity/.

Marine Mammal Commission. "Deepwater Horizon Oil Spill in the Gulf of Mexico." Marine Mammal Commission. https://www.mmc.gov/priority-topics/offshore-energy- development-and-marine-mammals/gulf-of-mexico- deepwater-horizon-oil-spill-and-marine-mammals/.

McGowan, Ragen. "15 Fun Facts About Dogs." Purina. October 4, 2024. https://www.purina.com/articles/dog/getting-a-dog/fun- facts-about- dogs#:~:text=While%20dogs%20often%20 urinate%20to,then%20 adding%20an%20exclamation%20 point.

McGruer, Dawn. "The Neuroscience Behind Business Growth." *Forbes*. September 2, 2024. https://www.forbes.com/councils/ forbescoachescouncil/2024/09/04/ the-neuroscience- behind-business-growth/#:~:text=By%20 integrating%20 neuroscience%20principles%20into,influence%20 their%20 development%20and%20motivations.

McLeod, Saul. "Pavlov's Dogs Experiment and Pavlovian Conditioning Response." *Simple Psychology*. February 2, 2024. https://www.simplypsychology.org/pavlov.html.

Mello, Juan. "The Peter Principle Explained: Flying Too High – When Promotion Meets Incompetence." *Management 30*. June 26, 2024. https://management30.com/blog/peter-principle/.

Millen, John. "Leadership Secrets from the Dog Whisperer."
John Millen.
https://www.johnmillen.com/blog/leadership-secrets-from-
the-dog-whisperer.

Mitchell, Andy, director. Inside the Mind of a Dog. Netflix,
2024. 1 hr 15 min.
https://www.netflix.com/watch/81681888?track Id
=255824129&tctx=0%2C1%2C59e3255a-bbbd- 4e9b-
b604-b514fdac547d-129333509%2C59e3255a-
bbbd-4e9b-b604-b514fdac547d-129333509%7C%-
2Cunknown%2C%2C%2CtitlesResults%2C81681888%2C
Video%3A81681888%2CminiDpPlayButton.

Mohtasham, Diba. "Guinness World Records posthumously
strips Bobi of his title of 'oldest dog ever'." NPR.org.
February 22, 2024.
https://www.npr.org/2024/02/22/1233186931/bobi-guinness-
world- records-oldest-dog-ever-title.

Mrs. Fields. "About Mrs. Fields."
https://www.mrsfields.com/pages/about. Pet Sitters

International. "Take Your Dog To Work Day® History &
FAQs." Pet Sitters International.
https://www.petsit.com/take-your-dog-to-work-day-history.

Ripley, Katherine. "Border Collie Facts You May Not Know."
American Kennel Club. February 6, 2024.

https://www.akc.org/expert-advice/lifestyle/fun-facts-
border-collie/. Rolls-Royce Motor Cars.
https://www.rolls-roycemotorcars.com/en_US/home.html.

Shea, Erin. "Why Do Dogs Wag Their Tails?" American Kennel Club. May 24, 2024. https://www.akc.org/expert-advice/advice/why-do-dogs-wag-their-tails/.